KW-278-069

The Spectre of Stalin

By Jean-Paul Sartre

SITUATIONS
WORDS
THE COMMUNISTS AND PEACE

THE AGE OF REASON
THE REPRIEVE
IRON IN THE SOUL
NAUSEA

BAUDELAIRE

TWO PLAYS
(THE FLIES *and* IN CAMERA)
THREE PLAYS
(CRIME PASSIONNEL, MEN WITHOUT SHADOWS
and THE RESPECTABLE PROSTITUTE)
LUCIFER AND THE LORD
KEAN
NEKRASSOV
LOSER WINS
THE TROJAN WOMEN
(*adapted from Euripides*)

The Spectre of Stalin

BY

JEAN-PAUL SARTRE

TRANSLATED FROM THE FRENCH BY
IRENE CLEPHANE

HAMISH HAMILTON

LONDON

First Published in Great Britain, 1969
by Hamish Hamilton Ltd
90 Great Russell Street London W.C.1

SBN 241 91317 9

Copyright © 1965 by Editions Gallimard

Translation copyright © 1969 by Hamish Hamilton Ltd

The Spectre of Stalin (Le Fantôme de Stalin) was first
published in *Les Temps Modernes*, Nos. 129, 130, 131,
November and December 1956; January 1957.
Reprinted in *Situations VII*: 'Problèmes du Marxisme',
2, Gallimard, 1965.

KING ALFRED'S COLLEGE
WINCHESTER

943.9
. SAR   38789

Printed in Great Britain by
Western Printing Services Ltd, Bristol

THE SPECTRE OF STALIN

[This essay, first published in Les Temps Modernes, 1956-1957, was prompted by the reactions to two events in October– November 1956 which caused considerable shock in the Western world: they were a Franco-British military landing in Egypt, and the Russian invasion of Hungary to suppress a rising in Budapest. M. Sartre here treats the Russian suppression of the Hungarian rising in considerable detail, but only refers to the Egyptian venture. The circumstances leading up to that were briefly as follows. The Suez Canal, completed in 1869, had been managed by the council (of international composition) of the Suez Canal Company (registered in Egypt, but with offices in Paris) under a ninety-nine years' concession from the opening of the canal (that is to say, it was due, failing a fresh concession, to come under Egyptian control in 1968). The Arab-Jewish conflict which followed the setting up of the state of Israel in 1948 led the then Egyptian government to hold up the passage through the canal of petroleum and other cargoes intended for Israel. Then, on July 26, 1956, without consultation of the company or of the countries represented on its council, the newly elected President Nasser of Egypt declared the canal national- ized. Long-standing border clashes between Egyptian and Israeli patrols came to a head on October 29 when the Israeli army in strength attacked Egyptian forces in the Sinai peninsula and swept them from the area by November 2. To separate these warring forces, a joint Franco-British air attack on Egyptian airfields began on October 31, and troops were landed by para- chute in the canal zone on November 5. Fighting ended at mid- night, November 6–7, following acceptance by Egypt and Israel of an unconditional cease-fire pending the despatch of a United Nations policing force to keep the peace. Nasser had mean- while blocked the canal with sixty-one sunken vessels and two

wrecked bridges. International units began to arrive on November 15, and British and French troops were gradually withdrawn during December. A Franco-British team began salvage operations in the canal on November 23, a United Nations group taking over on January 24, 1957, and completing the clearance of the canal by April 10, after which vessels began to go through the canal again, piloted by Egyptian pilots.]

I have received many letters recently. Among the questions put to me were two, repeated by very different pens, to which I believe a public reply would be useful.

1. 'By what right? . . . '

This one is addressed, over my head, to all Frenchmen who condemn Soviet intervention: 'By what right? In the name of what principle? of what philosophy? Of yours, without doubt. But you must understand that it binds only you.'

Some readers will, I know, be surprised that philosophical references must be insisted on before their detestation of this carnage can be permitted. Nevertheless, if they reflect, I believe they will find the question a fair one. Certain Communists have protested, and so has M. Denis de Rougemont: but it cannot be for the same reasons. The cards are so shuffled in this affair that suit and stake must be declared. This is proved by a chance distinction which has been hastily made: the Left condemns both the attack on Suez and that on Budapest; the Right only that on Budapest; *L'Humanité* only that on Suez. Strictly speaking, the links between the two massacres—at the heart of a world situation in which all events are interdependent—do not seem of the closest: the Hungarian rising surprised the Russians; the attack on Suez had been under preparation for several months. It may be that our political leaders precipitated the landing in spite of the advice of the generals 'in order to profit from Russia's difficulties in central Europe': I do indeeed believe them to be stupid enough not to have understood that Russia has the strongest army in the world, that it could crush Hungary and throw 200,000 men into Suez, that its difficulties are not of a military kind, and that it would be very happy to be able to raise its great voice high enough to cover the death-rattle in Budapest; but that doesn't take us far. Since then, M. Mollet and *L'Huma* have made the most touching efforts to establish a

2

profound link between these disparate events. M. Mollet declared, 'The Hungarians at Budapest, the French in Egypt have come up against the same arms';[1] and *L'Huma* said, 'The same Fascists demolished Port Said and hanged the workers of Hungary.' We have to admit the sad truth: today the French Left can define its position only by a double denial.

However, the two undertakings had this in common, that they were both of a political nature, and that they cannot be appraised without taking into account the objectives to be reached and the interests to be defended; in short, without making a political judgement whose repercussions can be only political.

I know M. de Rougemont: he is a gentle man, well brought up and into the bargain a Swiss: the military prestige of France does not dazzle him. It therefore seems probable that this 'European' considered the attack on Suez a sufficiently ominous blunder; nevertheless, he said nothing. Over Budapest, he has expressed himself at length. That is because he is anti-Communist: by preference, by chance, by profession. Now, his condemnation remains purely and simply *moral*: he is indignant in the name of the rights of peoples. It is his silence that is political. Or rather this mixture of dumbness and pronouncements. He will never again touch the hand of a Communist intellectual: this, you may think, is a really idealistic reaction. Certainly not: it assumes an air of idealism, but its true significance will be apparent if we remember that Rougemont would feel no distaste in shaking the hand of Guy Mollet. Here is what one of my correspondents writes to me: 'Only supporters of non-violence can judge.' Which means to say that only those who put the refusal to shed blood above everything else have the right to take up a *moral* position. To be sure. But it is precisely because they condemn *political* action *a priori*. Now at last, Soviet and French leaders have the right to challenge them: these moralists did not defend France against Hitler, they did not resist under the occupation or, if they did, they denied their principles; politics is necessary and no one can dabble in it—not even the plain citizen who votes for a party every four years—unless he accepts in advance that violence, in certain events, is the lesser evil. I summarize the letter of an advanced socialist who puts the question very clearly: 'You are not a Christian, neither are the

3

Communists. Can you say to them, Thou shalt not kill? You do not believe, any more than they do, in the virtues of passive resistance, in conscientious objection, in absolute pacificism: have you any right to upbraid them with their violence? You believe—as they do—in the Rights of Man and the Citizen as abstract principles of the middle-class Republic: can you condemn the Marxists in the name of out-of-date guarantees which have never abolished wretchedness or exploitation?'

He is right: at the worst, to take up a *moral* position conceals a political operation; at the best, it does not accord with the facts and the moralist is beside the point. But politics, of whatever sort, is action carried out in common by certain men against other men; based on convergences or divergences of interests, relations of solidarity, like those of struggle and of hostility, define a total attitude of man towards man; immediate objectives grow clear through distant objectives; *praxis* is controlled by the judgements of value which it generates and which are indistinguishable from judgements of fact;[2] thus true politics contains implicitly within itself its own moral evaluation. And the best way of making a total judgement of the actions of a government or of a party is to judge it *politically*. By that, I do not claim that any French party has the right to judge any other. For more than a century, under forms which change in the course of history, one movement alone has drawn the exploited on to lay claim, for themselves and for everybody, to the possibility of full and complete manhood; one movement alone has exposed in all its reality and defined the middle class as the exploiting class when all the rest treat it as the universal class; one alone produces through and by action an ideology which gives it understanding of itself as well as of others: that movement is the socialist movement taken in its entirety. This movement is the absolute judge of all the rest because, to the exploited, exploitation and the class struggle are their reality and the truth of middle-class societies: it sees the deep meaning of working men and of operative processes because it cannot but tie them to the fundamental structure of history, because it is the movement of man in process of developing himself. The other parties believe that man is already developed, and that he is the abstract subject of middle-class property, a surly angel all of whose needs are filled; they cover up exploitation and parcel

4

out the class struggle into sporadic and single conflicts; their ideologists and their historians look everywhere for the meaning of history, except where it is: for this reason, they lack the means to understand the action of the exploited classes or to judge them; they move away from the power of judging themselves because they do not want to know the truth of what they do. For appreciation of a political understanding, socialism is an absolute reference: it understands M. Laniel who does not understand himself. Of course, this movement would not know how to evolve abstract principles or a programme *a priori*: like production itself, like the balance of forces, in a word like history, it is continually changing. It would be absurd to refer to Blanqui or even to Guesde in order to appreciate what is happening today; and if we come back to Leninism, which is much nearer to us and still alive, it must be reconsidered in terms of a situation that Lenin could not foresee. But the very development of socialism, the principles it lays down through everyday *praxis*, principles which emanate from the masses themselves, which it takes up again and sets out explicitly in its propaganda, the judgements it passes every day on its enemies, its real action, the concrete relation which links its immediate objectives to its distant aims: in short, the current totality of the movement offers us light with which to illuminate all undertakings, and in the first place its own. Its appraisements are right: the mistakes, the blunders, the momentary failures change nothing. History has not sustained M. Thiers's reading of the massacres of 1848 or of the Commune: it has justified the people's judgement, the interpretations of Marx and Lissagaray. It is socialism itself which can and must appraise the actions of Guy Mollet, the socialist, and of socialist Russia.

These conclusions would compel us to fall back into idealism if we had to confine ourselves to them. For socialism is never simple; it breaks up and offers resistance to itself. In France, for example, the two great working-class parties, in spite of occasional all too brief truces, have fought one another since the Congress of Tours; they differ in their method of recruiting, in the trade unions they back as well as in their electoral supporters, in the interests they represent, in their political activity, in their programme, in ideology, and in their estimates of values which, born of their *praxis*, react on it in the form of

5

check or corrrection. It would be gratuitous for us to rely on the effective policy of one or of the other; we should, like the militants, be rapidly led to digest, at our choice, Suez or Budapest, if not by conviction, then at least through loyalty. It would be ingenuous to look for a community of principles between them which they do not possess and to base appraisement of their behaviour on some universal socialism which could be reduced at bottom to idealistic eclecticism. It would be presumptuous and vain for us to create, to fit the needs of the cause, an abstract theory which we might call 'true' socialism or 'pure' Marxism: the right reply would be that made by my correspondent: 'That is your philosophy; no one shares it.' Nevertheless, we must come to a decision: we are judged and defined by our judgement on the respective affairs in Egypt and in Hungary. To begin with, then, we will say that Communism appears to us, in spite of everything that has happened, to be the sole movement which still carries within it the likelihood that it may lead to socialism. But, in the current phase of Soviet enlightenment, violent contradictions rend the USSR and the people's democracies, oppose these to that, throw the CPs of the West into a state of crisis. At the root of these conflicts are the economic changes taking place in the East, and the upheavals accompanying them. This immense movement of organization and disorganization, of integration and decompression is translated, at the leaders' level, by absolutely contradictory undertakings, and by extraordinary shillyshallying. These undertakings are conducted simultaneously by groups opposing one another or representing the ever widening swing of a leadership which is united but, tossed ceaselessly from Scylla to Charybdis, is incapable of getting beyond the objective contradictions. If they take part in this conflict, men of the Left *here* must serve a policy continually called in question and fought against *over there*, which frankly accepts the current metamorphosis so that it can direct it and lead it to the end at not too great expense. So far as I am concerned, and in order to reply to my correspondent, I must determine in what political perspectives military action may appear the lesser evil; the very appraisement of these perspectives must then make clear in its major lines the socialist policy in whose name I have borne it, the only policy which is absolutely demanded and supported by reality.

So many precautions are not needed in judging M. Guy Mollet: he has never pretended to serve the cause of socialism. Truth to tell, he pretends absolutely nothing. This makes it easy to appraise his policy, that is to say to measure the distance between the decisions he takes and the living reality of the masses whom he represents and who voted for him. M. Duverger showed strikingly that anti-Communism and the slow degradation of the SFIO Party perpetually compel his parliamentary group to choose between opposition and treason. M. Mollet has flung himself into treason, and splashes about at ease in it. I know no one in history who has betrayed so many people at the same time.

His allies, first of all. Even before forming a government, he sacrificed M. Mendès France to the arbitrary demands of the MRP.

His electors next. They carried him to power because he had promised to make peace. Now, they have two conflicts on their hands.

And then, in general, all the people of France: he has caused the blood of soldiers to flow *for nothing*; he has disorganized the French economy by a criminal and half-witted lark; he has made the United Nations unanimously hostile to our country. He has shown everybody an abject France in which we refuse to recognize ourselves: cruel towards the weak, cowardly in face of the strong.

Finally, and above all—since this is what concerns us—*he has betrayed his party.* No one asked him to transform the country of M. Boussac into a socialist country by the stroke of a pen. At least he could have negotiated with the Algerians, carried out reforms in France, built houses. But no; this successor of Jaurès must suffer from myopia: he confounds the interests of the nation with those of M. Borgeaud, he sends the poor to violent death in order to defend colonialism and the big Companies; he puts at the capitalists' service that power given him by the support of wage-earners, he destroys at a single blow the pacificist traditions of his party by thoughtlessly throwing himself into a war of aggression. And what a war! An insidious propaganda murmurs without ceasing in our ears, 'Nasser the dictator! Nasser the dictator!' so that we may be persuaded that we are freeing Egypt from a tyrant. Nonsense! Our aeroplanes

7

have released their bombs on wretched peasants tormented by chronic famine. Nasser, in nationalizing the canal, was obeying the will of the people; with these new resources, he has constructed a barrage, irrigated the land of Egypt and increased its yield.[3] Mollet, in the name of the Suez Canal Company, caused the lightning to strike the insolent fellaheen: let them die wretchedly so long as the Suez shareholders get their dividends. By that same blow, he put the militants before a dilemma: they had either to leave the Party or to declare themselves in agreement with an undertaking they deeply condemned. Some left; those who remained, through loyalty to socialism, he degraded by attaching them to the British Conservatives; he subjected them to the contempt of the workers, their natural allies, and, worse still, to the approval of M. Duchet. This member of a caucus nursed the hypocritical illusion that he could draw a majority of the Right to the support of a policy of the Left: in the beginning, that is the illusion of all traitors. He has got over that: he is a traitor without illusions. But this experiment will cost his party dear: colonialistic, imperialistic, bellicose, our War Lord advisedly followed a policy of the Right with a majority of the Right. All along the line, the Right is winning: it reaches its objectives, and socialism is disqualified. M. Mollet will be given enough time to apply all those unpopular measures made inevitable by his mistakes; afterwards, the Right will burst this balloon and take power again amidst unanimous applause. At that moment, Fascism will be very near, and the SFIO will have been liquidated.

The 'blow of Budapest' is a different matter, and the questions it raises are of a different calibre; if we are to believe it, the government of the USSR intervened in *Hungary* to save the foundations of socialization there; it decided on this intervention the very day that the strength of counter-revolutionary troubles made intervention inevitable.

That is why one of my correspondents concludes, 'You pretend to be a socialist: be grateful therefore to the Soviets for having safeguarded, even by violence, Hungarian socialism.'

In short, I am reproached for isolating these massacres, for considering them in themselves, without taking into account the historical context, the compulsions, the goal. At Port Said, Mollet killed to defend capitalist interests: it is for that reason

8

and in that perspective that the Franco-British landing was to be condemned. But if we approve of defensive wars, wars of liberation, the 'maquis', the rising of oppressed classes, in short if, in certain circumstances, we accept violence, how reject it when the socialist structure is at stake, when armed Fascists are hanging Party militants, when the West is preparing to harvest the benefits of counter-revolution? To save the gains of the proletariat in Hungary is by the same stroke to protect similar gains in all the other people's democracies, and in the end in the USSR itself: the Red Army took up and continued in Hungary —with rather more imposing means—what the workers and sailors of Saint Petersburg began in October 1917; if socialism tolerated the shots of the battleship *Aurora*'s guns, why should it condemn those of Zhukov's tanks?

Such is the argument which runs in certain progressist and Communist quarters. It is said to be Marxist; I believe it to be much older than Marx; it can be summed up thus: 'What must be must be!' Each man explains it according to the particular delicate gradations of his sensibility. There are the brave ones who smile pluckily and say, 'Yes, indeed, there were some deaths. So what? Is the number of human lives that world revolution costs the one thing you consider? It's got to be done, you see. We must put up with them, these dead; it is our duty.' There are some sensitive people who have not closed their eyes since November 4 and who weep indiscriminately over brave workers hanged by Fascists and innocent proletarians struck down by Soviet bullets—wasted bullets, to be sure; in tears, they talk to you about 'the tragic dilemma', 'painful duty'. But if you ask them, 'But how about *you*? What is your own opinion of these events?', they move away with the air of being in a hurry, saying, 'I? Well, I'm bowled over, simply bowled over.'

There are the jolly fellows who laugh at the anger of others. 'But my poor friend, keep cool: you are as resentful as a cuckold, to be sure.' These are sure of themselves; they will never believe themselves cuckolded, not anyway by millions of dead. There are aggressive chaps: 'Well, well, my poor friend, it's lucky for you you weren't head of the Hungarian government; today you would have been hanged, and Horthy would be in power.' There are the impartial ones—generally progressists —who have learned to distrust their own personal reactions:

9

'We must judge sanely, with cool heads: we must see what is coming. Socialism is an immense happening which is to be measured on a scale of centuries. In a few decades, no one will be sensitive to the anecdotal aspect of the massacres, and their necessity, carefully decanted, will be visible in all its clarity.' There are the dialecticians who shrug their shoulders: 'The Russians are supporters of world peace? and they abuse Hungary as though they were deaf? So what? That proves there is still another contradiction in the progress of socialism; the only thing to do is to water it down.' One of these writes to me, 'Why break with our comrades over an action, deplorable certainly but entirely justifiable if an instant, the instant of truth, which exists today, is accepted? This is a new contradiction between socialism and peace, a contradiction which is not resolved by the doctrine of classical Marxism.' And then there are my two correspondents: 'In the name of what do you judge?' They all shelter their embarrassment behind this reasoning: socialism first; we will kill if it is necessary to kill; and may the blood of the innocent victims fall back on the criminals who pushed them to rebellion.

On one point we are in agreement: part of the blood shed drops back on to the Western governments, on Mr Truman's government. Beautiful souls, tender souls who wax so very indignant today in the columns of *Le Figaro Littéraire*, did you know that, day by day, radio stations, whether or not subsidized by the United States, incited the Hungarians to rise when the West had neither the means nor the intention of supporting them? Yes, indeed, you did know that: it is concealed from no one and middle-class newspapers congratulate themselves on it. Did you protest? No: you approved of this propaganda, or rather you were irresponsible, conceited, above all, frivolous, and you passed over in silence the havoc it might wreak. Well, read today in the *middle-class* press (in *France-Soir*, for example, and in *L'Express*) the reports of their special correspondents: you will learn that the Hungarians spit on our flag. Those who, away there, thought these broadcasts ill-omened and mendacious are at one today with those whom they encouraged; in vain you will offer them all your large, magnificent hearts: they meet your outpourings with hatred.

That said, I consider the argument of those who are upset and

10

of the grumblers at a glaring fallacy artfully supported by un-proved assertions; it would have to be proved to us that social-ism was lost without Zhukov's armour. Now, the facts reported to us—true or false, in general false rather than true—simply assert that it was in danger. To accept this assertion, that Russian intervention saved socialism, is to put the USSR be-yond attack: necessity compelled it to strike, it re-established the situation, that is all; an objective disorder set automatically compensatory mechanisms in motion. No one among these enthusiasts was willing to understand that the USSR *by its actions defined* its own socialism and the socialism it counts on re-establishing in Hungary. No one has dared to ask himself if this military action, in restoring through the balance of forces the internal relations of the socialist camp, has not more gravely injured the cause it was defending than free elections and neutralization would have done. No one has noticed that the intervention *was the expression of a policy*. In order to answer my correspondents, it is necessary therefore to reconsider every-thing, and to begin again at the beginning.

Let us concede for a moment that the intervention was not inevitable. The regular government, therefore, recognized its powerlessness: after twelve years of absolute power, it had lost control of the masses and no longer represented them. Its lone-liness, the hatred felt against it even in the ranks of the Com-munists: these are the true reasons for its call to the rulers of Soviet Russia. Foreign intervention thus appears like the logical conclusion of an abstract and false policy which led to economic catastrophe, and which of itself was bound to generate counter-revolution. That being so, we refuse to consider and to appraise separately the last link in the chain. Over-industrialization and accelerated collectivization *were already criminal: from the first day* they carried within themselves the massacres of Budapest as their outcome; these massacres, if the right to condemn them at the time they occurred and from the day they began is with-drawn from us, we shall condemn them from the first day of 1949, for they were already present, they soiled in advance all the proceedings of blind leaders. What does it matter, in fact, what a government believes it is doing? What counts is what it *is* doing. And what was it doing? It was systematically pushing an entire people to despair. I am obliged to compare those who

11

come to tell us, eyes starting out of their sockets, of the diaboli-
cal power of the Fascists, with Mr James Burnham, known
specialist in anti-Communism. Reading his books gave me a
good laugh: he showed us prosperous workers bound to their
employers by community of interests, by reciprocal esteem; a
state of bliss. And then, suddenly, risen from hell, a handful of
Communists appeared, stirring up discord everywhere: that was
all that was required to cast a happy people into despair. I have
found similar arguments from Communist pens: the only difference is, they did not make me laugh. And then, no, to be just,
there is another difference: in a socialist country, the workers
must have community of interests with the circle of the leaders.
But if they have it, if they eat at their ease and if the standard of
living rises, if they are aware of working for themselves in working for everyone, is it to be believed that Fascism could persuade them they are dying of hunger? And if they don't have
this community of interests, whose is the blame? I do not under-
estimate the rôle played by the exiles. I say that people do not
cheerfully let themselves be killed when they can avoid it; I say
that Fascist propaganda is not enough to throw them, unarmed,
into an attack against armour, and that, for people to court
death, they must see nothing in life but a prolonged agony: I
shall not have the impertinence to remind the Communist
leaders of the motto of the silk-weavers of Lyons: 'To live working or die fighting.' Nevertheless, I know they will find it apt.
And they are right. But what were they saying about the Hungarian workers?

These workers, strangely enough, annoy certain of our Stalinist intellectuals. Some have taken the line of systematically
denying their existence, like that gallant bastard who said to me
yesterday, 'Budapest? A detestable town, nine hundred thousand small shopkeepers earthed up in their holes.'[4] Others, more
enlightened, do not dream of denying that the Hungarian proletariat exists, that it took part in the rising, elected workers'
councils, and decreed a general strike. But, for that precise reason, our 'tough guys' do not see it in a favourable light. Already
M. Stil has begun the good work: these committees, these
factory councils, eh? You know where they come from, and
who elected them? Come, come! They're under the control of
the Fascists. That's well known, in Budapest. The very next day

12

Kadar loudly gave him the lie by accepting them as representatives of the working class and agreeing to negotiate with them.[5] But already the argument has travelled some way. And someone was grumbling the other day, 'The working class? Well, so what, the working class? Do you believe it's infallible? Did it budge when Louis Bonaparte carried out his *coup d'etat*? Were there no workers behind Mussolini? Behind Hitler?' If I had not heard these remarks with my own ears, I should not dare to repeat them. And, of course, it must be admitted that the working class is not infallible if by that it is understood that no one is possessed of infallibility, that the truth is established little by little in the dialectical relationship between masses and leaders, in the midst of blunders and costly mistakes, by means of discussion and sometimes conflict. But we shall refuse to follow the Communists who denounce the blunders of the proletariat when their real aim is to argue that their political bureau is *invariably* in the right. It is all very well, in fact, for the bureau to denounce the blunders of the masses when it has declared Kostov, Rajk, Slansky in turn to be criminals in white shirts, to be guilty, when it has denied the existence of labour camps, when it has proved that Tito was a Fascist 'in the scientific meaning of the term'! I know what it will say, as its members are saying day after day: 'Mistakes have been made, but. . . .' Only that particular 'but' cannot be accepted. Mistakes have been made. That is all. Linger a while on that, M. Fajon. Draw certain consequences from it, for yourself and for your friends. This, for example: that at present it is necessary to be modest, very modest; that Mr Khrushchev has uncovered your lies before the whole world, and that it is better to wait a little while before starting to put them about again. And then, you see, the Hungarian workers have been able to deceive themselves *politically*—it is you who say so, and for the moment I am certainly willing to admit this. But when they said, 'We are overworked, we haven't enough to eat', they provided the positive gauge of what was too much and what was too little. In refusing to listen to them, the Rakosis, the Gërös—these friends whom you still defend, in private—proved to them that the policy of the Party was false, that the bureaucratic apparatus under-estimated the revolutionary strength of the masses and took no account of their aspirations; it was their mistakes which made the working

13

class understand that, *even in a socialist country*, it was under an obligation to create its own organs of defence.

When everything is weighed up, French Communists must be advised not to shout too loudly that Soviet intervention could not have been avoided. For this pious argument carries the most radical condemnation of everything that has been done in Hungary up to this very day. Torture, faked confessions, false actions at law, labour camps: these acts of violence are in any event unpardonable. They might have been forgotten, later on, if they had been only the dross of an immense upheaval, of a society in process of laying the foundations of socialism. But when everything crumbles away at the same time, when—if you are to be believed—the whole people takes the Fascist side in order to liquidate the régime, the foundations of socialism have never existed. How heavily they weigh, then, all these crimes committed for nothing, all these useless sacrifices; the failure of the Stalinists shows up in their true light this wretchedness and this terror, the only future of which was the final catastrophe.

But I do not altogether share the irresponsible severity of our Stalinists. I recognize that agricultural collectivization had miscarried magnificently, that industrialization remains a semifailure. But through all that, nationalization of industry has brought forth its fruits: a working class has been forged which wants to defend socialism. And this sentence from a Communist friend who is much attached to the Poles could very well be applied to the Hungarians: 'In Poland, the motor car industry has produced poor cars and wonderful workers.' No, the consequences of Stalinism were not *fatal*: de-Stalinization ought to have been carried through in time. If, in 1955, Nagy had continued in power, if he had been recalled even at the beginning of October 1956, the rising would not have occurred. The people were pushed to the limit by the explosive mixture, at the heart of the Party itself, of a still aggressive Stalinism and of supporters of de-Stalinization; thence came the hesitation, the flashbacks, the shillyshallying, the contradictions. Do not let us forget that Khrushchev, in this same month of October, landed at Warsaw while Russian and Polish troops under Rokossovsky were marching on the capital: if, at that moment, Geroe had been in Ochab's place, we should be shown today that Russian intervention was necessary in Poland, we should be hearing

14

about Polish Fascism. Conversely, if Ochab had been secretary-general of the Hungarian CP, *Pravda* would have celebrated Hungarian-Soviet friendship, and have presented it as an example to the countries of central Europe. And, undoubtedly, it will be said that Gërö is the product of Stalinism: that is true. But so also was Ochab. No, the die is not cast once and for all; struggle is necessary. But if the spilling of blood could still have been avoided in the first fortnight of October, who can persuade us that it was unavoidable at the precise moment it took place?

As we have seen, those who take the necessity of Russian intervention for granted, adopted a definite position at once, on the basis of no information whatever. They are not interested in Hungary, but in the USSR. And their firm belief is born of an act of faith: '*Since* the Red Army cannot fire on the workers without absolute necessity, the massacre at Budapest must have been necessary.' For them, the socialist structure of the USSR decides its relationship with the socialist countries which surround it, and those relations cannot but be socialist. Now, the Communist Parties of the whole world, the Movement for Peace, the Soviet leaders have condemned a hundred times the principle of military intervention, and proclaimed the right of peoples to self-determination. *Therefore* the Soviet army has *in reality* intervened only against foreign agents: it brought help to an allied government and to the working classes, it saved good Communists from massacre, fought the Trotskyite demons and the Arrow Cross, encouraged the masses to thrust aside temptation; as for the shots fired, all that need be remembered is that these lightning flashes provided enlightenment to a people in doubt and showed them the way; guided by the historical process, the shells selected Fascists, and struck no one else.

The trouble is that the Army of socialism shed blood at least once without the least necessity: in Hungary, precisely, some days earlier, when it first intervened. As we muse, with no evidence, on November 4, that night of October 23–24 is entirely forgotten: then, at Gërö's appeal, the Soviet command agreed to throw its troops against the crowd. Today no one dares to pretend that at that moment there was any question of a 'Fascist *putsch*'. Even M. Waldeck-Rochet acknowledges that the first troubles expressed 'a legitimate discontent' among the workers. The crowd in the streets, both jolly and angry, less

15

angry perhaps than jolly, was not sure whether it was *demanding* the return of Nagy or *celebrating it in advance*: the central committee had not yet come to any decision, but, in the eyes of the masses, that decision was taken for granted. Had it been proclaimed at once, calm would little by little have been restored. Gërö, on his return from Belgrade, furious at having been humiliated in front of Tito, behaved like a *provocateur*: can he have been unaware that, in treating the demonstrators as though they were a rabble, he would at one stroke change a demonstration into a riot? Who knows, perhaps that is what he hoped! Who fired the first shots? Demonstrators? The AVH? Followers of Rakosi betting on the worst? No one knows. But what, on the other hand, we know only too well is that Gërö jumped at the chance and called the Red Army to his aid. Only, Gërö was no more than a supernumerary. Can anyone be persuaded that the Russian leaders were obliged to obey him? Could they not, on the contrary, have pointed out his failure to him and advised him to disappear? Recalled during the night, Nagy would have had every chance of quelling the riot *if* the Russian troops had not been in such a hurry to open fire. Put into office by the Soviets and under their protection, Janos Kadar does not hesitate, today, to speak of the crimes of Gërö and of Rakosi; his protectors permit him to talk: are we to believe that their soldiers fired on the people at the appeal of a criminal, and in order to cover up his mistakes? Better still: Nagy has never hidden what he thought of the appeal to the Soviets; responsibility for it has been attributed to him, and he defended himself fiercely against this accusation: 'It's the Rakosi assassins who want to blacken me,' he said. Now, Kadar was a member of the government and has never protested; if he resigned on November 2, it was for other reasons which we shall discuss later on. He is still trying hard today to justify the events of November 4; but he never reverts to those of October 23. Implicity, that is a denunciation of the step taken by Gërö as a gratuitous crime, in which the Russians acted as accomplices. And the Soviet government? What has it to say about the matter? What do the Soviet writers say about it in the message they have addressed to us? Nothing. Absolutely nothing. This first massacre was so great an embarrassment to MM. Garaudy and Waldeck-Rochet, the editors of *L'Humanité* and of *La*

16

France Nouvelle, that they consistently behave as though it had never happened.[6] Action by Fascist commandos, the lynchings, the landslide to the Right—all the facts, more or less interpreted, with which they make play—took place *after October 24*; they are attempting to justify *the second intervention*. But I will not weary myself by repetition: it is the first intervention which must be considered first, it is of this that we must speak. And, when the Stalinists try to prove to us that the second aggression was inevitable, our answer is that if that is so, it was the first which made it necessary. O you sanctimonious knaves who brag of having killed so as to avoid a world war, when it was by your first murders you ran the risk of provoking it! You pretend to have saved socialism: yes, on November 4. Though, indeed, that is disputable: but when you fired, in those days of October, when the armour of the Communist Army at the appeal of a Communist leader massacred Communist workers, your shots and your shells smashed socialism itself to smithereens.

In politics, no action is unconditionally necessary. Even after the 'landslide to the Right' of the Hungarian revolution, armed repression could be considered as necessary only in a certain perspective which takes for granted certain immediate as well as other more distant objectives, a certain technical connexion with these ends, certain values, a conception of man; nothing more is needed to understand that this perspective results from certain groups, that it reflects their structure and their interests. In order to assert that, in the Hungarian affair, respect for 'non-intervention' might have brought about world war, it is necessary to accept a certain idea of the people's democracies, of Western capitalism, of the balance of forces, of the class struggle. In relation to these hypotheses, a certain future must have been backed; a policy in relation to that very future and to the revolutionary strength of different proletariats must have been defined. This implies that certain information is available and is appraised in a certain way, that is to say in relation to certain set purposes and a certain culture. But this culture and these set purposes define in their turn the men who have made the political choice: they send us back to their basic attitude towards socialism and towards man, hence to their character, to their interests, to the class or environment which produced

17

them. As regards events in Hungary, only one question need be asked: for whom and in what political perspective was Soviet intervention necessary? We cannot answer it without first trying —so far as may be possible—to decide the nature, the composition, and the development of the insurrectionary movement between October 24 and the morning of November 4.

Announcements by Radio-Budapest and, shortly afterwards, certain admissions by the Communist leaders make it possible to separate two extreme positions: even the Communists recognize today that it was not simply a question of a Fascist *putsch*; only the Trotskyites insist that the insurrection was wholly of a Left-wing character. The truth lies somewhere between these two equally unfounded and schematic assertions. Somewhere, but where? To find that out, a Marxist analysis of the position would be required: but its elements are still not clear. Fajon, Garaudy, Waldeck-Rochet repeat in chorus: 'Let us be Marxists!' But, after some commonplace catechismal observations on post-war Hungary and on its evolution since 1945, they stop abruptly. Because they know nothing. All they can do is to hold forth on the class struggle; it seems we have 'underestimated' it. Now, the class struggle exists: it is the driving force of history. But there is no need for the Political Bureau to harp on it continually. You will have to come to terms with this some day, you lazy and light-minded Marxists: a people's rising in a socialist country forms no part of your schemata. And you are so well aware of this that you are playing the fish: in Hungary, what you call the 'class struggle' is the exploitation of the revolt by foreign capitalism. Your absurd reasoning is reduced to a series of false equivalences: the cold war is only a form of the class struggle;[7] anything that might be useful to the Western *bloc* is by definition counter-revolutionary; now the Hungarian rising—whatever its aims, its factors, its activating causes— played into the hands of capitalist imperialism. Therefore it was a counter-revolution. These unmanageable Hungarians who detested the tyranny of Rakosi's followers under-estimated the class struggle; these nationalistic Communists who want to establish true socialist links between the USSR and Hungary under-estimated the class struggle. And hunger? And the chronic weariness of the workers? These exigencies pushed under-estimation so far that they led to a lowering of produc-

18

tivity and sabotaged socialist planning. But tell me, this Rakosi, in fact, the man who has got you all into trouble: did he not under-estimate a little? Wasn't he by any chance an American agent? And you know the power of the Right, you who live surrounded by reactionary, wicked, crafty controversialists who are prompt to underline your weaknesses, don't you under-estimate the class struggle when you serve up to us the most imbecile falsehoods, when you excite the laughter of the whole of France, when you quietly leave out of your newspapers news which is in everyone's mouth? When M. Stil writes cheerfully that Budapest is smiling again, and when Mr Nehru, quoting from his ambassador's report, declares that the aspect of this city is 'heart-rending', which of them, in your view, is the better anti-Communist propagandist? Mr Nehru or the editor of *L'Humanité*? Wouldn't you also be a little, just a very little, counter-revolutionary? The class struggle: words which indicate a moving and complicated reality, always present, often difficult to decipher, you twist them forcibly to mean 'the hand of Uncle Sam', and you stoop suddenly to the level of an imbecile Right which sees 'the hand of Moscow' in every strike. Those who do not suddenly discern American parachute troops amidst the wretched crowd, you treat as lower middle class. To speak truth, this insult is astonishing: what are Communist intellectuals if not members of the lower middle class who have placed their pens at the service of the working class and who, though they have become Communists, continue to live like members of the lower middle class? But no: that is to be ill acquainted with them. These intellectuals have what we lack: the reflex action of class. Evidently it can act only as a conditional reflex since they are very rarely sprung from the proletariat, and since things are so arranged that they never come into touch with it. But each time they learn that an innocent Communist, such as Rajk, has been hanged, or when a working-class crowd is fired on, as in East Berlin, at Poznan, in Budapest, this news produces among them an abundant secretion of the salivary glands accompanied by repeated cries of 'The class struggle! Unity!'

In *L'Humanité* of November 30, I read some remarks from the pen of Laurent Casanova which at first seemed to be more relevant and which then foundered suddenly in paranoia: 'Any analysis of events is incomplete which neglects or impugns the existence and activity within the people's democracies of social forces hostile to revolutionary changes, organized by and dependent on world imperialism, which makes use of them with the object of internal subversion and war against the socialist camp.'

I follow him and I approve of him when he speaks of 'social forces hostile to revolutionary changes'. And then, suddenly discouraged, I find my approval slacken when he speaks of 'forces organized by world imperialism'. To begin with, I don't know what 'world imperialism' is: inside the Western *bloc* there are *some* imperialisms which are in general opposed to one another, witness the 'attack on Suez'. If what is meant is American imperialism, that should be stated: it would be clearer. But this line of thought can do no more than handle symbols; it is as far from the truth as the Hungarian CP was from the masses. In such a case it does not matter what historian should try to determine what were the counter-revolutionary forces, what strength they disposed of, who organized them. M. Casanova leaves all that in the dark. I shall speak of these forces in a moment. As for their organization, what does he know? Exactly what we know: there is the Kerstein amendment and its 'thousand million exiles', there are the appeals of 'Radio Free Europe', there is the 'National Committee for Free Europe'. These are propaganda weapons; their origin is very diverse; their aims and their financing are also diverse. There exists at Munich a radio financed by the State Department which is directed at the Russian people. But 'Radio Free Europe', so far as I can judge from the information at my disposal, is maintained by the exiles themselves;[8] and the programmes emanating from this dispensary are so varied that the Polish station was beseeching Poland to 'remain calm' in those same October days when the Hungarian station was urging Budapest to rise. As for the 'extraordinary Committee for the transmission of arms to Hungary', it would be vain to call it to account: it was formed *after* the rising. Quite. In any event, this propaganda is inexcusable, its effects have been disastrous. But it is only propaganda. Are you not aware that 'American imperialism' has always hesitated between two policies: that of 'containment' and that of 'pressing back'? That these two policies correspond to groups of divergent composition and with divergent interests? That 'containment' has always *in fact* prevailed? That this uncertainty in American policy, sometimes encouraging the exiles, sometimes abandoning them, produces as a consequence a very real paralysis of their activities? That the exiles themselves are corroded by internal conflicts, by often relentless struggles among themselves? Why, if you are aware of all this, do you present world imperialism to us as a sure and indivisible force which goes straight to the point and brings off the impossible? For I am, after all, familiar with counter-revolutionary propaganda, and I willingly admit that it is accompanied by spying. But you will not make me believe that, *in the midst of the Rakosi terror*, it would have been possible to organize and arm commandos on Hungarian territory; whence were the arms to come? Were they dropped by parachute? That was possible in France, during the Occupation, because the whole country was behind the Resistance. But in a country as divided as is Hungary, it is altogether outside probability. You really suggest that in a dozen years, Rakosi had never heard speak of this secret militia? That when he put Rajk on trial, he did not seize the opportunity of denouncing these supplies dropped by parachute?[9] And who trained the counter-revolutionaries to handle modern arms? Where did they carry out their drill? In the country districts? But the troubles broke out in Budapest. The commandos had already moved there? We shall come back later to this hypothesis. I will only recall some facts: when the AVH, in the approaches to the Parliament house, began to fire on the crowd, *it had no arms* and was so numerous that the first ranks, wedged tight by the pressure of those behind, had to endure the gunfire without being able either to take flight or to defend themselves. It was at this moment that the students went to beg the Hungarian soldiers in their barracks to come to the rescue. The soldiers still hesitated (they joined the rebels later); but, after a moment, the gates of the barracks opened, and four lorries full of arms made towards the Parliament house. Where, then, were the American missiles? And where was the organization? The French CP, bemused by the 'cold war', thinks only in military terms: if certain reactionaries take part in a riot, it sees them immediately in steel helmets, carrying flame-throwers and bazookas. When will it understand that these conceptions spring

21

not from Marxism but from mythology? When will it understand that facts must be assembled before they can be explained,
that the Marxist method permits the interpretation of experience, but not its suppression?

Not immediately, of course. The following more theoretical
paragraph from Casanova's article filled me with amazement
and made me despair of official Marxism. It begins well enough:
'It is necessary to take into account two essential factors—the
mistakes of those taking part, and counter-revolutionary activity
—and unite them in an analysis set in the perspective of the class
struggle.' Nothing could be better. But wait a little: 'The thought
process which would see only one side of the question or would
establish between these factors an hierarchic order is a risky one
which may well falsify the whole analysis.' No hierarchic
order? What may that mean? We determine the conditions of
an historical fact and, what is more, pretend to *unite them in an
analysis*. Why is it necessary to forgo the determination of their
respective importance? In mechanics, each force acts as if it
were the only force; but in an historical perspective it is necessary to consider the reciprocal action of the factors, to study the
modifications which each of them produces on the others: is this
possible without noting from moment to moment polarizations,
regroupings, the perpetual play of dominant and of recessive
forces: in short, a moving hierarchy of conditioning factors?
When Marxism says of a class on the way up that it is the
subject of history, does he not establish an hierarchy? When
L'Humanité congratulates the Red Army on having prevented
world war, is it not establishing an hierarchy? What can result
from this strange decision to adopt two different and equally
incomplete explanations, and to develop them in parallel while
pretending to unite them, without ever comparing them or
bringing them into touch? By the negation, pure and simple, of
all dialectic. For real forces, isolated concepts of understanding
are substituted; two abstractions are presented at the same time
—the 'mistakes' of the Government and the forces organized
by world imperialism in the unique design of balancing the first
by the second, and in the end of finding once more the classical
schema: Right-wing opportunism will exaggerate the importance of the mistakes; sectarianism, on the Left, will charge all
to the account of imperialism.

22

Marx would have made fun of these pompous asses who take the class struggle for a Platonic Idea or who make it intervene like a *deus ex machina*. Even acquaintance with the earlier facts and with the structure of the new society—acquaintance which, besides, MM. Casanova and Fajon totally lack—can illuminate only imperfectly a process which has its own history and in the course of which relationships have not ceased to evolve. What must be shown are the real contradictions of the Hungarian rising, and the shifting relations which they set up between the classes. Let us try.

The most obvious fact is that, until October 23, the demands made rested essentially on democratization. Nationalism was in abeyance: the followers of Rakosi[10] had exalted it in words and degraded it by every one of their actions: this treatment had added to its strength in the hearts of the people. But perhaps he was afraid to show himself in his nakedness: he would then have appeared as a terrible negative power; hatred of the occupier would have carried him off. Happily, social claims allowed him to express himself without uncovering himself; he was the sinew and the first condition of democratic reforms: could Hungary seek its own way towards socialism without first rendering up complete sovereignty to him? The most concrete and the most immediate claims opened out directly into a national exigency. How raise the standard of living without making a change in the distribution of investment, that is to say without establishing plans of production with the co-operation of Hungarian experts alone? How give the trade unions their true function if norms of authority and of routine were fixed according to Russian demands? It seemed therefore that Communism in Hungary could not be saved without completely reconsidering the relations of Hungarians and Russians.

It is on this social basis that all who laid claim to democratization leaned vaguely. This unity concealed divergences of interest and of perspective: for the Communist opposition, it was above all a question of getting into touch once more with the masses: sovereignty, however desirable it might be, seemed to be the chief means of revalorization and of working towards experience; for the conservative lower middle class,[11] on the contrary, democratization was the means, national independence the end. On the other hand, the members of the CP

23

wanted to loosen Rakosi's vice-like hold, revivify the Party, get back 'to Leninism', but they did not for a moment envisage any modification of the One Party system. By contrast, the Social Democrats and the Smallholders had no conception of democracy except as a return to a plurality of parties.[12] These divergences did not stop there: certain among the members of the old non-Communist groups, sure that the CP would oppose all electoral consultation, were content with effective participation in the Government; others continued to intend to insist, in due time, on a return to the parliamentary system. These a little later were compelled to divide over a question whose urgency had not yet become apparent: was it necessary to reconstitute only the parties which were represented in the government in 1945, or should older factions be resurrected, new formations be permitted to come to birth? In the first case, the *liberal* principle would be arbitrarily restricted: in the second, under the pretence of complete liberalization, lay the risk of opening the door to Fascism. But, in the universal confusion of the first fortnight of October, these attitudes were neither clear nor well marked; they might co-exist or succeed one another in the same group, in the same individual. What they all had in common was rejection of Rakosi's dictatorship and, in depth, the demands of the nation.

In the Writers' Union, in the Petöfi Circle, the movement of the intellectuals had been above all *critical* and *negative*: it withdrew into more and more violent opposition instead of constructing positive projects of government; the situation made *that attitude* necessary, and no other. The function of the intellectuals was to represent negativity: it was not a question of proposing to Rakosi that he should carry out certain changes for the better in the system; his crimes had to be revealed to everyone, so that he could be totally discredited and compelled to resign. As we know, they succeeded. If their criticism had an undeniable influence on the working-class masses, that was precisely because it was negative. Events in Poland showed the course to follow: before any other change, the national Communists, who could negotiate with the USSR, must be united and carried to power. The whole country clamoured for Nagy. This Communist had a splendid part to play. Programme, methods, rhythm, the scope of democratization: nothing had been defined. The immediate objective was strong and precise claims but these obviously had to be set out in the perspective of practical possibilities: the writer who denounced Zhdanovism, and the worker who claimed a rise in his real wages, both contributed to determine the direction and the content of democratization. A complete policy still had to be elaborated on these data, and it had to take into account at the same time Russian dispositions, Hungarian aspirations, the economic situation, and counter-revolutionary threats. That is what gave M. Nagy his chance: for the Hungarians, democratization had to be blended, at least to begin with, with the action of a sincere government having political experience at its disposal, able to rely on experts and technicians, and competent enough to envisage the problem in its totality. By putting itself at the head of the reform movement, by telling the whole truth, by going beyond certain claims, by explaining to the country at once why other demands could not be satisfied immediately, the Nagy government could enhance the influence of the CP and diminish that of the Social Democrats; sincere and total *democratization* made *liberalization* impossible.

In the night of the 23rd to the 24th, the whole set-up toppled over. Democratization took a back seat; Soviet aggression provoked an explosion of nationalism. On the previous evening still, all these people were seeking agreement on a political and social programme: they were working together at the heart of a United Front, spontaneously formed, whose immediate task was to fight the aggressor. The Russian intervention drew their bonds tighter, crystallized their latent anti-Sovietism, stirred up the already excited people, gave it other aims, essentially negative. In this revolt, there is no need to see either blind and disorderly reaction or a movement organized by a single directing force. M. Garaudy can be reassured: there was no question of spontaneity. Years of oppression had forged these men and the bonds that united them. The unity of the Party, of its methods and of its terror had given rise in the people—despite divergence of interest—to the diffused unity of rejection. It was a question of identical, unorganized, but not solitary reactions: no individual had any need to speak in order to know that his personal attitude was that of everyone else. Among us French people, exploitation leans on disintegrating forces: a continual effort is necessary to keep up unity. Rakosi's dictatorship, on the other hand, in aiming at securing integration by violence, had brought the workers closer, but it had brought them closer *against the dictatorship*; in uniting them by false relationships which masked their dependence, it had made them aware of their true relations. These relations rested midway between real unity, which assumes the organization of a diversity, and identity, simple co-existence of similar particles which know nothing of one another: it was, if you like, the deep but unrealized knowledge of a negative identity. This is what explains the original character of the rising: it was sporadic, confused, with no underground strength; no secret direction had prepared it. But this apparent disorder covered a new-born order: each group of fighters was aware that it represented the whole people, precisely because its particular reaction was a particularization of the general reaction. In order to appreciate this, there is no need to know the details of episodes in the battle: for each insurgent, these scattered fights were always *national*; they contained the promise and demonstrated the need of unity in revolt. Each group chose its own leaders; in a very little while, those in a position of responsibility established contact with one another: some among them acquired considerable influence (the one to whom most attention was paid was Maleter, a Communist). But the rising remained to the end a hydra with a number of heads. And it is true that one adventurer, tempted by Fascism, with his men—some of whom were Communists—occupied the premises of *Szabad Nep*. But he withdrew very shortly without having molested the journalists and, two or three days later, at the first conference of the units in revolt, the leaders present broke with him unanimously save for one vote.

The Communist newspapers have often referred to the presence of armed exiles, but they have given no proof of such presence. There was vague talk of American arms, but it was without conviction. And among the prisoners? No least foreign agent? In Berlin, some Germans who had come from the West were picked up: their photographs were published, a case was got up against them. Nothing of the kind in Hungary: but how convenient it would have been! What's that? On the 23rd, the Red Army occupied the town and cut it off from the world; on the 30th, it quitted the town, and it did that in order to encircle

26

it. The presence of Soviet troops certainly might not have put a stop to infiltration, but made the arrival of massive Fascist reinforcements very unlikely. Peter Fryer, the Communist correspondent of the *Daily Worker*, reported a piece of information he had been given by some Austrian Communists according to which, before November 4, 2,000 exiles, armed and trained by the Americans, would have entered Hungary. Did these Communists know what they were talking about? From what eyewitnesses had they got their information? No one knows. And if I report this fact, it is out of consideration for the personality of Fryer who wrote, as is well known, articles turned down for their excess of good faith. In any event, this is the sole indication worthy of examination that we possess. And, even if we are willing to accept it, it is to be observed that 2,000 exiles, even armed, are quite incapable of changing, by themselves, the course of a revolution. For the rest, since we cannot check the information about them, I must point out that according to the *New Statesman*'s correspondent, whose reputation for honesty is well established, up to November 4, those frontier posts in the hands of the insurgents drove back all the exiles who planned to re-enter Hungary, and in particular Ferenc Nagy, the leader of the exiles. There are said to have been some commandos. Communist observers have assured me that this was being said in Budapest. It was being said because those who repeated it had heard it said. But these same observers had perambulated the town in all directions without ever meeting them, or meeting anyone who had actually seen them at work. We should remember those 'brigands' who, at the time of our Revolution, were seen everywhere and were nowhere. For many Hungarians— above all for those of the Left—the memory of 1919 and of the White Terror has not been wiped out. They believed they were re-living their past. And even if they existed, these commandos, were they any danger to Democracy? Let us think rather of the others, of the immense majority of the insurgents, workers, students, soldiers, men of the lower middle class: no one today would any longer dare to call them Fascists, *not even* M. Waldeck-Rochet. M. Stil notes with disdain the extreme youth of the fighters (teddy-boys, as it were): this contempt sits wonderfully well on the representative of an outfit with hardening arteries which can no longer make recruits among the young,

27

and whose middle-agedness rises year by year. But his remark turns back on him: in 1945, in a Hungary, divided, ravaged, crushed by years of Fascism, on whom could the régime count if not on the young whom it was going to form? It has had twelve years to attach the young to itself, and the only result of its efforts has been that it is the young people who are the most eager to knock it down. How pedantic and scholastic their masters must have been! How over-simple and stupid must have been the Marxism taught! Among the students there are some whom Stalin has disgusted with Marx: deprived of all contact with Western culture, they have no other ideology to replace it; they turn towards their national literature which was always political and which has reflected for more than a hundred years the aspiration for independence of the people. Certainly they are not nationalists and *only* nationalists; some of them have stayed *with the Left*. But their hatred of bureaucratic despotism extends to the principles to which their tyrants appeal. Above all, they want *certain liberties*: that of speaking and expressing their thoughts, that of offering criticism, that of being kept informed, that of joining together according to their inclinations. They do not believe that these entirely legitimate claims can be supported by a Marxism of which they have been shown only the authoritarian aspect; so that these claims gave rise among them, as in certain writers, to an unconscious return to a kind of anarchism.[18] No doubt this tendency could be dangerous, but only in the long run. It leads to indiscipline rather than to Fascism; and that indiscipline, so long as fighting continued, was obliterated through the voluntary discipline of the fighters. And then there were the others—the best, perhaps—those from whom the cramped catechism of the Stalinists had failed to conceal the immense possibilities of Marxism. These fought to save culture.

In the name of Rakosi's followers, it was socialism that many lower middle-class people fought, consciously or not. But they were not very numerous among the insurgents; besides, it would be a serious mistake—I am sure M. Casanova will not make it —to confound with them the members of the apparatus, the trained personnel, who lived in a homely way, and of whom some, nevertheless, took up arms. And above all, it is an undeniable truth that workers made up the majority of the fighters.

According to the statements of a Hungarian trade unionist whom leaders of the CGT met in Prague, it seems that the workers in the industrial suburbs had no arms to begin with. That is easily explained: the rising broke out in the centre of Budapest. As I have said, the first deliveries of arms were made hastily from the barracks to the crowd: among all this crowd, there were some workers, but there were also, and above all, students and people of the lower middle class. These first supplies rapidly exhausted the most accessible stocks and, for some hours or some days, the labour force of the great factories was obliged to remain empty handed. But it has been proved today that Nagy undertook to arm the proletariat systematically —probably through the medium of the trade unions—in order to oppose with authentically revolutionary forces an eventual return to reaction. No one, surely, will dispute Marshal Zhukov's evidence: on October 30 he said, 'I consider the fact that it gave arms to the workers proves that the new Hungarian Government did indeed depend on the working class.' Unfortunately for him, the working class made use of these arms to defend the people of Hungary against the Soviet soldiery: it was at Csepel, *in the homes of the workers*, that the battle raged; it was there that it lasted longest. What should we think, here in France, of a rising which developed above all in the 'red girdle' of Paris? Should we dare to call it Fascist? Here is the point at which we are presented with the sweep of spontaneity. You are well aware, says M. Garaudy, that the proletariat must not be abandoned to its spontaneous reactions. That is very true if by this we are to understand that the working-class movement must make up its mind from day to day through a consistent dialectic which puts trained personnel over against the masses in order the better to unite them; that the first, by education, by sincere explanation, and by agitation, must struggle against dangers from the outside; that the second, as soon as they are on the march, go beyond their leaders, dragging them along as they themselves radicalize their claims. But all this no longer means anything if it is to be argued that a socialist government has the right to repress by force the rising of a proletariat which it has reduced to despair. For after all, if we abandon myths and symbols, what did Lenin want to say when he spoke of spontaneity? That, quite simply, *in a*

29

capitalist country different factors—among them we might mention the actual condition of the worker, fear of bloody repression, the ideological propaganda of the middle classes, the forces of massification—lead the worker without political education to put his hope in reformism.[14] What meaning does the theory preserve when it claims to be applicable to the armed revolution of a proletariat in a socialist country? Marx explains that the revolutionary force of the worker in middle-class societies 'is born of the contradiction between his human *nature* and the conditions of his life which are the evident, positive, and total negation of that nature'. In spite of the socialist form of Hungarian society, no one would dream of denying that that contradiction continued to exist within it; besides, proof of this will be found in the evidence which follows this article. Where does spontaneity come in here? It must, in a socialist country, incline the proletariat in the strongest way to reformism.[15] It is not therefore spontaneity which pushes the masses to armed insurrection, *it is necessity*. I am very much afraid that one of the major contradictions which gave birth to the Stalinist system cannot be covered up under the name of spontaneity: that is, the contradiction between need and the plan. We shall come back to that. Certainly the composition of the Hungarian proletariat is far from being homogeneous. Out of 1,600,000 workers, rather more than a third has been tapped by the super-industrialization of the 1950s. To measure the unbelievable rapidity of this demographic upheaval, let us recall that Budapest rose *in six years*—1948–1954—from a population of 1,058,288 to one of 1,700,000. These newcomers, taken aback by the brutality of methods, by the rapidity of changes,[16] undoubtedly retained, in varying degree, their peasant mentality. Perhaps some of them, delivered over to their 'spontaneity', that is to their village routines, allowed themselves to be tempted by political adventure: but they were in a solid framework of older workers who had known the Horthy dictatorship and who were endued with genuine revolutionary traditions. These proved fighters were joined by the young people who had come into industry immediately after the war, between 1945 and 1948; at that period the rural exodus was slower, norms of work were lower, changes less abrupt: without difficulty, they identified themselves with the working class. It is true that, before 1939, the

30

most combative kernel of the proletariat was Social Democratic, and that the CP scarcely existed. But do not let us betake ourselves to thinking of our Guy Mollets: the Party, unlike ours, represented the proletariat, and not the lower middle class; it was a question of *tough* Socialists formed by a dangerous and painful struggle against government by a dictatorship. In defiance of its official disappearance, the influence of Social Democracy had been preserved, and the criminal imbecility of the Rakosi régime had reinforced it; in spite of bureaucratic tyranny, shortage of manpower and the effect of rapid industrialization neutralized bureaucratic dictatorship: ill nourished, badly housed, overworked, spied on, the workers, despite their dumbness, knew their weight, were well aware of their true importance. Crushed by degrading propaganda lies, by police inquisition, they felt themselves valorized at a new level by the extreme need for them which existed. So that the contradictions of the régime fortified their courage and their class feeling. They took up arms to overthrow a tyranny which was leading the country to ruin, but never—whether they were Communists or Socialists—did they question the socialization of industry. They had long accepted the need to sacrifice themselves for socialist Hungary; they rebelled when they saw that these useless sacrifices prevented neither the decay of the nation nor the liquidation—sooner or later—of its socialist bases. Whatever we may think of the burst of indignation in Budapest, and of what might have come of it without the intervention of November 4, it is impossible to insist too strongly on the crucial fact that characterized it: the workers were unarmed, they had no desire to restore the factories to the capitalists—what folly could have pushed them to that?—but, as the event proved, they wanted to ensure control of industry by electing joint production committees and workers' councils. It was these workers' councils, constituted in the first days of the rising, which never ceased to function, which transformed armed resistance into a general strike; they it was which, in several provincial towns, put an end to reactionary troubles; they it was which compelled Kadar to negotiate with them. After the crushing of the revolt, they were the only living force, at the same time socialist and national, which opposed the Russians and the reconstruction of the bureaucracy. Who, then, would dare to deny

31

that they represent a past positively in favour of Hungarian socialism? In particular, I should like to ask those Communists who are still hesitating whether this strike, prolonged in spite of terror and massive arrests, these negotiations continually broken off, continually taken up again, about which Radio Budapest speaks from day to day, do not, by their very nature, throw serious doubt on the counter-revolutionary character of Hungarian resistance? Soviet newspapers pretend that the Red Army intervened at the side of the workers against the insurgents. The workers inflict a humiliating denial on them: their strike, and the maintenance of their claims, prove that they have been and that they continue to be with the insurgents and *against* the Red Army.

Whatever the risks and mistakes of this crushed revolution may have been, the working class of Hungary has taken it to itself, and made itself its heir and its guardian. Who then, when the Russians themselves are compelled to admit to negotiations in Budapest, who, among the leaders of the French Communist Party, will dare to challenge the evidence of a whole proletariat?[17]

However, from October 23 to November 1, the slide to the Right is undeniable; the situation deteriorated. Again, we must be precise: this change was not caused by the abrupt appearance of Fascist demons sprung from no one knows where; it was a result of the lack of balance within the insurrectionary movement, a kind of internal metabolism which tended to modify the structure of its groups and the balance of forces among the fighters.

The principal reason for this evolution must be sought in the circumstances of the first Russian intervention. Hungarian officialdom had long since lost its standing among the masses; the Communist Party was suspect. But, in spite of eight years of tyranny, of shocking or ludicrous mistakes, of crimes, the chances for a national and democratic communism remained intact. The masses are realists: at the beginning of a strike or a revolution, they claimed the *minimum*, an improvement that would make very little difference to their condition. It would have seemed, even to the Social Democratic workers, unreasonable and absurd to demand the liquidation of the CP: it was well known that the Soviets would have no confidence except in a

32

Communist government, and that a Communist government alone could negotiate with them. On the 23rd, some hours before the rising, all the people of Budapest were out in the streets. But it is too often forgotten that the opening demonstration took place in honour of Poland: the events at Warsaw, the Polish victory of October 18 had deeply moved the Hungarians. Perhaps some of them were fêting Gomulka *in spite of* his adherence to the CP, but, whether they intended it or not, their compliments were addressed to a Communist. This vast festival is the proof that the masses were asking for government *à la* Gomulka in Hungary: nothing more, nothing less. Besides, Social Democracy was virtually out of commission: for the workers, it was a tradition of struggle, a way of life. Unorganized opposition, it had for some years profited by the people's discontent; but its frontiers were shifting. Many of the workers were both Communists and Social Democrats. And then, above all, it was incapable of presenting a constructive programme: Marxist, it was at one with the CP in defending the bases of socialism, and at one with the Communist opposition in calling for democratization. If Nagy, recalled on October 15—and perhaps even on the 23rd—had taken immediate steps to raise the standard of living, to stabilize norms of labour, and to endow the workers with genuinely defensive agencies; if he had proclaimed his willingness to re-organize the national economy; if, like Gomulka, he had disclosed with no reservations the extent of the disasters to be overcome, and had offered general lines for a plan of reconstruction; if, finally, he had announced that he was opening negotiations with the Soviets, he would have dealt a terrific blow to Social Democratic opposition by taking from it its reason for existence. In a word, all could have been saved, and to begin with the Communist Party itself.

But is was Gërö who was governing. In calling for the intervention of the Russians, through a fool's mulishness much more than from cowardice, he had at a stroke put the CP out of court; the first discharge of the machine-guns made it irreparably the party of the foreigner. That was false: a great many of the militants, mixed in the crowd, unreservedly approved of the demonstrators; Hungarian Communists fell under the shot of Russian Communists. This criminal folly was only an involuntary jerk of dying Stalinism. But for the crowd—and on the morrow, for the whole country—all this occurred as if the CP had revealed its true face; the insurgents could see in it only the savage instrument of Soviet oppression. At once, nationalism became fused with anti-Sovietism and anti-Communism. The Communist opposition had, however, won over the insurrection; its members had been well received, some of them had acquired influence over their comrades: but they had been listened to *by virtue of* being insurgents and *in spite of* their adherence to the CP. Nagy himself was discredited: he had been called on when all was lost and had made the mistake of accepting power without laying down conditions. Above all, the responsibility of the call to the Soviets was at first attributed to him. He denied this. In any event, it is true that he had not sent out the call *in so far as* he was head of the Hungarian government. But, said the insurgents, Gërö had got his criminal decision approved by the Central Committee, and he had collected a unanimous vote: moreover, Nagy had been present. To which his sparse supporters replied: he was present at the sitting of the Central Committee because he had been summoned to attend it, but he was not yet a member; his election to it was carried only much later. Perhaps it was hoped to compromise him: if so, the manoeuvre succeeded. It must be added that he was, for the first days, virtually a prisoner of the Central Committee, in which Rakosi's followers were in the majority: that explains why he had at first[18]—gently—disapproved of the rising instead of taking the lead in it and giving it a programme which would have allowed its canalization. Through this ambiguous attitude, he lost his popularity for a moment. When he shook himself free from ambiguity, it was too late: this government, called for for too long, contaminated by a massacre of which it was innocent, displeased the Soviets without pleasing the insurgents. The Soviets reproached it with giving way to pressure by the people; the insurgents with promising what it would not be allowed to carry out. The contradiction is clear: a Communist government was necessary to undertake democratization with the consent of the Russians, and to push it through without abandoning the principles of Marxism. The only possible government was thus Nagy's; but from the night of the 23rd to the 24th, Gërö had undermined Nagy's authority. The pro-

34

visional disqualification of Nagy faced the insurgents with an
unexpected situation: the abeyance of power. At the same time,
Soviet shells shattered Marxism, and this brutal liquidation of
the dominant ideology left the insurrection without a programme and without resources. United in a national struggle,
the insurgents had not yet found a common denominator for
their claims; no political judgement came to enlighten their
struggle; the insurrection took place without self-recognition.
In the west of the country, it seemed that reactionary forces
must triumph; everywhere else the majority wanted to protect
the social conquests that had been made. But ideological uncertainty was liable from minute to minute to break the front of
the insurgents and throw them against one another. In certain
parts of Budapest, armed workers made ready to fight at the
same time against the Soviets, against the AVH, and against the
armed groups which would have liked to call nationalization in
question. The links between the trade unions—organs of the
Rakosi dictatorship—and the workers' councils were far from
clear. In the trade unions themselves, opponents of the system
came into conflict with the bureaucratic majority. The trade
unionist of whom I spoke earlier summed this up in a single
phrase, 'Everybody was against everybody else.'

This situation could not last: at all costs, divergences had to
be overcome. This is what, among some, transformed the will to
democratization into the demand for *liberalization*. The only
people who could, in fact, substitute themselves for the Communists were the Social Democrats; but first of all they had to
be recognized as a party. And how could the reconstruction of
this party be claimed without at the same time demanding a
reconstitution of all the other dissolved formations whose old
members were fighting side by side with them—in particular, of
the Smallholders' Party? But as for this party, whose very name
is a programme, it was made by agricultural socialization
which, besides, the peasants had already undertaken to
liquidate. And how prevent the appearance or reappearance of
other political forces? Would it be possible to forbid the Catho-
lics, who had already liberated Cardinal Mindszenty, from
forming a group? In this extreme confusion in which Marxists
were fighting against Marxists, in the name of what were the
principles of Marxism to be abandoned? And the small trades-

people, the still numerous craftsmen, who had never rallied to the régime? They might well be held to be class enemies: but that did not prevent them from paying with their blood for the right to express their opinions. As often happens in wars of liberation, the class struggle gave way to the struggle against the foreigner. From the moment he took up arms, every Hungarian tacitly received from the other insurgents the right to put forward his point of view, immediately and later on, after victory. And these men with divergent, sometimes actually opposed, interests could remain united during the battle only if they agreed to demand an electoral conference: only elections could set up and guarantee peaceful rivalry among their representatives.

Rakosi's régime was neither a Fascist dictatorship nor some other kind of tyranny: in spite of everything, it represented socialization; it simply represented it badly, which is worse than not representing it at all. The suicide of this monster left an unfillable void. By violence, by terror, he had integrated all classes into the régime: the insurrection had necessarily to present itself as a disintegration. Of necessity, forces, masked or long pent-up, made their reappearance. Deprived of free will by the breakdown of the CP, the insurgents drifted towards the Right in order to maintain the unity of their fight; the immediate exigencies of the struggle imposed on them the need to demand a return to a parliamentary régime. On the morning of October 30, the situation was altogether paradoxical: there was still a government. But already the USSR refused to place any confidence in it. As for the insurgents, they looked on it as an abstract power whose unique office it was to validate their demands. Under their pressure, Nagy kept re-shaping his ministry in order to reproduce within it the image of the insurrectionary groups; but, by that same token, he lost his whole reason for existence, for in truth he was neither the opponent of the insurgents nor their emanation. Thus, always outflanked, always late by an hour or by a day, this government was obliged to gather speed: it was in the tow of the insurrection. At each new concession, the Soviet leaders felt their distrust reinforced: they regarded Nagy as a traitor. In fact, he was a sincere Communist whom the course of events was in process of *decommunizing*. A Communist leader, in fact, depends on a well constructed

Party which, in theory at least, ensures links with the masses. But the Party had faded away. The Central Committee was in hiding, the militants were handling guns in the midst of the insurgents. When they negotiated with Nagy, the representatives of the insurrectionary groups never addressed themselves to the Communist, but to the nationalist leader of a government of transition. That was the whole misfortune of this good and sincere man: subjectively, he remained faithful to his Party; objectively, everything happened as though he had deserted it. Suddenly, after having aimed at liberty in the bosom of the régime, the masses demanded the liberty of setting up for themselves a régime that pleased them.

Therefore it is correct that the insurrection turned to the Right; that is not to say that Right-wing elements took the lead in it, but that the struggle against the foreigner created of itself conditions which might some day allow them to seize power. Free elections—blameless in principle—might have led to a majority of Smallholders in a new Parliament.[19]

Equally, the suicide of the CP changed the nature of the national demands. Certainly the fight of the insurgents against the Soviet troops could have only one meaning: they demanded the departure of the Red Army. This departure itself must have inaugurated a new phase in the relations between Hungary and the USSR. But *neutralization* is only one very special form of return to sovereignty. There are other more positive, more fruitful forms: for instance, an alliance proclaiming at the same time the independence of the countries signatory to it and the community of their interests, which means that they would reconsider together and on an equal footing their economic, political, and military relations. When the Party governed, many people reproached it with servile obedience to the USSR: for that precise reason, this same Party, renovated, democratized, with new and national leaders, might have served as a real and effective intermediary between the Hungarian people and the Soviet government. In all the people's democracies, in fact, Communism and nationalism are in deep contradiction; the national Communist is a man who has lived this contradiction, who has been forged by it, and who tries to get round it without giving up either of these two terms. For this reason, Gomulka saved Poland without breaking with the USSR. For

37

this reason also, the disqualification and breakdown of the Hungarian CP broke all concrete relations between the two countries and destroyed all organs of mediation: this Party, in fact, when it was dictatorial, headed and itself directed, under the control of the USSR, every sort of undertaking, whether economic or cultural. Because he had suppressed those organizations and public authorities which enjoyed the confidence of the USSR, the criminal folly of Gërö had the effect of shutting the door to all negotiated solutions which the USSR might have accepted, Nagy, no longer a true Communist, did not represent the Party in the eyes either of the Russians or of the insurgents. Between Hungary and Russia, there was only one remaining relationship: battle; the middle course had failed. Some insurgents, some Russians: that was all. The first could not conceive of independence except in its most immediate form: that is to say, above all, in the departure of the second. And neutralization only reflected back this exigent demand. The links once cut, what could the Hungarians have demanded if not coexistence in its most elementary and most negative aspect: that is to say, in short, juxtaposition pure and simple? It goes without saying that they sincerely believed in calming the misgivings of the Soviet leaders by undertaking to maintain the same relations, or the same absence of relations, with their neighbours to the West. Neutralism, in itself, cannot be considered as an attitude of the Right, and elsewhere the USSR has shown itself favourably disposed towards it. But the USSR had approved of it to the same extent that it enfeebled the enemy *bloc*. Neutrality in Hungary: would this not be economic competition, *on Hungarian soil*, between East and West; would it not, in short, be a victory for the USA and, who knows, for the return of capitalism? That, at any rate, is what the Soviets very sincerely dreaded.

Such was the evaluation of the situation in the last days of October: the self-destruction of the CP imposed a negative programme on the rising. And this negative programme—free elections, neutralization—might, if it were accepted, take Hungary back into the Western *bloc*. They are lying, those who pretend to explain the slide to the Right by an invasion of exiles, or by the abrupt re-emergence of counter-revolutionaries who had concealed themselves within the country. It was very pre-

38

cisely the opposite: if certain reactionary elements were able, here and there, to make themselves heard, it was the abrupt vanishing into thin air of the CP which made this slide inevitable, in spite of the insurgents themselves.

It must be added that, from the 31st, the departure of the Russian troops provoked an abrupt decompression—an explosion of joy, of hatred, of violence—which impelled the crowd to lynch members of the AVH and, probably, a few Communists.[20] At the same time, Cardinal Mindszenty spoke on the radio. His pronouncements made it seem that he considered himself the inspiration, if not the leader, of the forces of reaction.

Was the position of socialism and of democracy desperate? That is what it is hoped we shall be made to believe. But let us look at the matter more closely. First of all, these lynchings were atrocious. But we are being made fun of when an attempt is made to hypnotize us over them and to give them political significance. All the same, it must not be forgotten that Rakosi's was a police régime, and that the AVH had made themselves detested as much by the Communists as by the 'reactionaries'.[21] But *above all* it is sought to conceal from us an essential fact: which is that during the night of the 23rd to the 24th, they gave the signal for the slaughter. Very often the Russian soldiers hesitated, sometimes they fraternized with the people. The AVH did not hesitate; they took their time, took careful aim, and fired. That is what the crowd did not forgive them: Hungarians, they had opened fire on unarmed Hungarians. They should have been brought to judgement: agreed. But history provides a thousand examples of such lynchings: they are the effect of simmering hatred and of fear turned into aggressiveness; it is the paralysis of authority that makes them possible. Today, it is sought to attribute responsibility for these summary executions to Horthy commandos. In the past, the Girondins tried to get it believed that the September Massacres had been organized: by Marat, said some, or by Robespierre. Others said, by Danton. Still others, by the Commune of Paris. Today's historians are agreed in considering that they were the result of a collective movement. Brought to a standstill by mutual distrust and hatred, the only responsibility of the Legislative Assembly and of the Commune in regard to them was that they could not prevent them. In Budapest, Nagy was powerless; the insurgents, to

39

begin with, were reluctant to oppose the people: could they, in their turn, open fire on them? Their only means was to gain the people's confidence, but that required time. This slow but firm action bore fruit: as soon as the insurrectionary committees had taken things in hand, the number of lynchings diminished; on Saturday, the 3rd—the eve of the Soviet aggression—order had been completely restored. As for Cardinal Mindszenty, the Stalinist press made a bogy of him. But we need more than a repetition of the words of an old man worn down by suffering and shored up by his grudges to discover behind him an army of Fascists ready for action. On what forces did he depend or believe that he depended? He had been cut off from the world for eight years, then, abruptly, liberated: can we believe that he had a clear idea of the situation? Between this hollow voice drifting over the radio waves and the carnage carried on in the gutters, the Communist press sought to see a deep relationship. Those who believed this did so through violent emotion; only Stalinist paranoia prevented them from seeing the truth: which was that this old, remote priest and these head hunters were separated by an immense void. The evolution of the Hungarian rising depended neither on the one nor on the other. I know: the influence of the Church is deep: later, during the holding of elections, who knows if Mindszenty might not have stood surety for the party of the counter-revolutionaries? Yes, who knows? But who knows whether his intransigence would not have disquieted Rome and turned the majority of believers against him? Nothing can be decided on this point; neither among us, with the meagre information at our disposal, nor even in Budapest where the game was not played.

In fact, on the eve of the second aggression, Saturday, October 31, positive elements were numerous. The middle-class press and *L'Humanité* are in agreement in juggling them away: the first because it is bent on its 'Saint Bartholomew of the Patriots', the second because it wants to see in the Hungarian drama the wonderful uprising of suffocated liberalism. These elements must, therefore, be underlined.

All the countries of central Europe have not the same structure: they all pass through a difficult spell, but they do not encounter the same difficulties. After 1945, the Czech government, for example, found itself faced with a serious problem:

industrial progress between the two wars had led to a considerable increase in the non-producing classes; these had to be integrated into the new society, to be resorbed little by little. I do not believe that this has been altogether carried out, or that this middle class will ever rally to the régime; it is knowledgeable, capable, and to be feared. For its own advantage, it would run the risk of juggling away a national insurrection against the Communist leaders, or of transforming it into a civil war. Still, it is true that the proletariat is also very strong there. In any case, events at Prague would take another course, even if they started as they did at Budapest. Before the war, a Hungarian middle class had scarcely begun to develop: far from constituting the preponderant social force, it could hardly be reckoned one of the *leading* classes. Middlemen, in terror of the great landed proprietors, had not dared to carry out their 'middle-class revolution' or to endow the country with a national industry; on the contrary, they favoured the development of foreign undertakings. Hungary found itself in the hands of great ground landlords; its natural resources were exploited by various strongly industrialized countries: Fejtö called it a 'semi-colonial nation' and with good reason. The 'tertiary' group has never developed there: the hostility of a national upper middle class depending on the lesser middle classes which it has developed, a plethora of higher civil servants and administrators who, although wage-earners, are completely loyal to capital: that is the worst danger with which a young socialist state can be faced in its beginnings.[22] The Hungarian state was, in advance, spared this danger. The upper middle class had always been weak and cosmopolitan: emigration and purges broke it down, and it had altogether disappeared. There was no reason to fear that it would seize hold of the operating levers or that it would deflect the rising. The Hungarian lower middle class, made up of tradesmen and craftsmen, does, it is true, present certain conservative tendencies; but, in any event, these could not be compared with the will to exploit which characterizes the capitalist class; with them, it is simply a question of deep attachment to individual ownership. There can be no doubt that this small-scale ownership (of the street stall, of the shop), still to a considerable extent tolerated by the Hungarian leaders, can expand normally only in a society of capitalist structure where the play

41

of competition, giving an advantage to some at the expense of others, leads to concentration. But just this type of society has never succeeded in becoming established in Hungary, and anyhow, it is no more than a memory or a dream: where could forces be found capable of restoring private capital? This lower middle class vegetates, clinging to its remaining privileges rather than dreaming of gaining new advantages:[23] it remained under Rakosi what it had been under Horthy: its 'class viscosity' is so considerable that sons do not try to raise themselves above their fathers, at least not unless they become Communists and enter government service. What changes everything, in fact, is that there is, above this class, a social group which possesses comfort and middle-class power, which might perhaps act as a lure to it: that is the socialist bureaucracy. Authority and riches come to it through its adherence to a practice and an ideology which are repugnant to lower middle-class people. I have never thought of bureaucrats as a class. I even find this categorization totally absurd: it remains none the less so because in Hungary high officials and even simple political police spies enjoy scandalous privileges. So that the Hungarian rising put wretchedness and want against opulence. It was not *at first* the principle of private ownership that the lower middle class, alongside the workers, was defending. The contradiction of this reactionary class was that it was fighting against privilege and against luxury, in the name simply of the right to live. Also, whatever may have been its distant and subjective aims, it was defending objectively a more equalitarian socialism alongside socialists and against corrupt socialists.

As for the big ground landlords, they had emigrated: had they wished to return, with the help of disorder, on what support could they have counted? The country people, on the announcement of the rising, had redistributed the co-operative estates; they had, in short, destroyed the socializing exertion of the Revolution. But in this liquidation they did not revert to the state of things in 1939; these unfortunates—of whom the oldest had never, up to the war, worked except on the land of others—found themselves owners; they took over from the régime its first reform, that sharing out of the land which might be called 'middle-class'. If the Nagy government had agreed to this NEP, if it had accepted the failure of rapid collectivization, not with the idea of remaining indefinitely against change but of beginning socialization again slowly, cautiously, the Hungarian peasants would have found themselves in the position of those who acquired national goods at the time of the French Revolution; they would have defended the régime, as our small owners defended the Republic, because they, like the French peasants, would have dreaded above all the return of the exiles. Cardinal Mindszenty was very well aware of this since he began by declaring that he accepted without reservations the nationalization of the property of the Church. Moreover, in the country districts there were hardly any troubles (Soviet troops were, for the most part, busy in the great industrial centres); there is no mention of fights or of massacres; scarcely any settling of accounts. After this new sharing out of the land, carried out everywhere with the consent of all, the peasants were satisfied and went back to work. This new situation admitted of some risks: the co-operatives had not only proposed to increase productivity, they aimed also at preventing the reconstitution of large estates. But that danger was long-dated: a solidly established government could take severe measures, forbid the transfer and sale of lands, strike at the new kulaks by ruinous taxes. The Hungarian small landowner had allied himself with the kulaks against compulsory collectivization; he would ally himself with the government against kulaks who would like to ruin him in order to take his goods away from him: in both cases, he is fighting against expropriation.

In fact, the programme of the insurgents was never reactionary. It could do nothing but record the total failure of the co-operatives. That was right, that was prudent.[24] But, at Kilian barracks, while the insurrectionary leaders were in conference, one of them, a Communist, declared that, whatever happened, the conquests of socialism would remain; his proposition was accepted unanimously. He was aiming, evidently, at the socialization of industry. Besides, a little later the insurrection forced Nagy to accept as the point of departure a régime which scandalized the Russians, but which the errors of Rakosi had made necessary: the industrial sector would remain nationalized, the agricultural sector would be given over provisionally to small private ownership. I have described the dangers of this régime, and I have shown its necessity. The future was going to depend

43

on the parties and the men whom the insurrection would carry into power.

Now, after the false departure of the Soviet troops, the Hungarian fighters dreamed of re-tying their bonds again; to prevent the resurrection of old political groups or to limit the risks of electoral consultation, they envisaged the formation of a large Party of the Revolution which would gather in the Christian Right and the lower middle class, ex-members of the Smallholders' Party, Social Democrats and Communists. Negotiations were seriously under way when the Red Army made its very noticeable return. They had to be interrupted and arms had to be taken up again. No one knows whether these negotiations would have led to anything; and, even had they done so, no one can be sure that the party so formed might not have fallen to pieces. But, if it could have got the better of the contradictions within it, there is no doubt that it would have collected a majority of votes. Socialism would have gained from it: in a parliament elected on the basis of the 1945 elections, the CP and the Social Democrats had found themselves in a minority faced by hostile parties closed and impervious to their influence; they had formed the opposition—perhaps an ineffective opposition. By contrast, in the bosom of the great Party of the Revolution, no barrier would have separated them from the old comrades beside whom they had fought; they alone were possessed of experience, method, an ideology; they alone were possessed of a technique of propaganda and of agitation; they alone knew how to organize, how to govern; they alone aimed at distant targets through immediate objectives: thanks to these undoubted superior qualifications, they ought to have been able to exercise a decisive effect on hesitant men without political experience.

From November 3, the uniting of the insurgents began to bear its first fruits, and order began to be re-established. It was at this precise moment that the Red Army chose to strike. How can anyone dare to pretend that the tanks came back into Budapest to deal with a state of extreme urgency? We may well think that the Kremlin hardly gave a thought to the temporary anarchy which still reigned in this encircled town. What concerned it above all was the subsequent development of the situation and its repercussions. Now, there can be no doubt that the

44

return to calm would have marked the beginning of a hard struggle; the contradictions of an economy torn between the socialized sector of industry and the 'free' sector of agriculture would soon have put the towns against the country, the workers against the peasants; questions of supplies and of prices would have roused the anger of country people; if food prices were not regulated, the worker would have gone hungry. From this clash the middle class would have profited to set itself up as arbiter; but within itself the middle class carried its own contradictions: belonging to the town, it had the same needs as the proletariat: an authoritarian policy in relation to food supply and prices would have served its interests; conservative, it would have allied itself with the rural classes in defence of private ownership. In the country districts, as I have said, a great deal of dexterity and cleverness would have been necessary to prevent the new kulaks from exploiting or expropriating the poor. On cultural grounds, Marxism, still powerful but a little discredited, would have been faced with alternative ideologies generously offered by the West and, who knows, with a sudden recrudescence of the Christian faith. It is the whole of these clashes of interest, and not simply the cock-and-bull tales of *L'Humanité*, that deserve the title 'class struggle'. Workers, the lower middle class, peasants, kulaks, smallholders: it is on the confrontation of these forces, on the complicated interplay of their alliances and, of course, on relations with the USSR and with the West, that the fate of Hungary depended. And so what? Doesn't it depend on the same things today and won't it so depend tomorrow? The Russians can do nothing about it. Did the class struggle come to an end under Rakosi? Wasn't the withering away of the co-operatives one of its effects? Was the ascendancy of Christianity relaxed? And did the workers, in spite of the discouragements that deluged them, cease for a moment to want socialism? Vexation and great dangers can produce momentary unity; brutal force can sometimes crush divergences: but it is always necessary to get back to politics, to commit oneself to uncertainties, to take risks, to feel confidence in certain classes and to depend on them. The Soviets have always underestimated the revolutionary power of working-class movements; in the Hungarian affair, they suddenly noticed the slide towards the Right and took no account of the simultaneous reinforcement of the

45

Left: distrust is not dialectical. Nor Manichaeism. The Soviet bureaucracy doesn't like workers in arms: it very much prefers soldiers to them. On November 4, it wagered on the triumph of the counter-revolution against the Marxist revolutionaries. The struggle which began might perhaps, it is true, have ended in civil war; but it might just as well have led to the true dictatorship of the proletariat. For the working class was armed; and it had to hold on to its arms: the insurgents wanted to form, after the departure of the Russians, a national guard composed of students and workers. This, in short, would have been made guardian of nationalized industry. What strength these men, who had not been intimidated by Russian armour, might have shown against exiles and counter-revolutionaries! After the crushing of the rising, on November 16, a representative of the factory committees spoke on Radio Budapest asking his comrades to return to work, on conditions. He spoke like a conqueror, with wonderful pride: the strike was to be ended so as to go to the help of the inhabitants of Budapest; it would be resumed immediately if the strikers' demands were not satisfied. And in a building stuffed with police, in a ravaged town where Russian tanks were on patrol, he added these words, 'The whole world knows our strength.' We know it, it is true: one million six hundred thousand workers can keep the most powerful army at bay. Are we to believe that those men unaided were incapable of stifling counter-revolution? It was certainly necessary to take some risks, to get organized, to define a policy, to look for allies: these men were ready for all that. Was it therefore so foolish a project? And which is of more value for the Country of the Workers: to blow up a capital, decimate a people, ruin an economy already close to failure, or to have confidence in a conscious and armed proletariat? A struggle had necessarily to be foreseen: yes, but was it a *genuine* struggle, that of the real forces of Hungary; would the clash of classes have burst out into full daylight? Undoubtedly, but what was to be gained by masking it? Would the USSR have been present, powerless, at the crushing of the forces of the Left? And why? Could it not have befriended them? Agreed to give substantial help to a government in which the Communists were largely represented? It serves no purpose to stop by force the free development of a country: it must itself overcome its own con-

46

tradictions. But, it will be said, what about the exiles? the commandos? the West? Get away with it! The USSR has just crushed Hungarian resistance, and not a country of the West budged. A distinguished speaker even said the other day, to the Movement for Peace, 'Why do we worry about Hungary? No one is going to war for the Hungarians.' This speaker was a Left-winger, and the Communists applauded him. Is it to be believed that the USSR cannot negotiate with the USA? Impose total neutrality on the West in return for its own? Declare that it would hold the Western states responsible for any armed groups which might form themselves within them and attempt to cross the Hungarian frontier? Proclaim that it would send two hundred thousand 'volunteers'—as it did over Suez—should armed exiles enter Hungary? The chatterers of the West made themselves detested by the Hungarians whom they pushed into revolt in order afterwards to abandon them to their fate: however strong anti-Sovietism may have been, couldn't the USSR reckon on anti-Westernism? If it had drawn back its troops, would it not have regained—in part at least—the ground it had lost? Ah! that would have been to take risks. Yes. But does anyone by chance imagine that still greater risks were not taken by having recourse to force?

No one has the right to say that events in Hungary made intervention inevitable. No one: not even those who decided on it. For the rest, blunders and repentance, false departures, returns,[25] this strange paralysis of the troops faced by the strike; the announcement of deportations put out by Radio Budapest itself and contradicted next day; the strange comings and goings of trains crammed with prisoners being taken towards the frontier 'for questioning', and subsequently brought back; the 'slide to the Right' of the Kadar government which seemed at one moment about to revive all the concessions made by Nagy (except neutralization), then its abrupt hardening; the deportation of Nagy and his ministers; the out-and-out rejection of the workers' claims, followed very soon by resumption of negotiations; then the dissolution of the committees:[26] all this combines to demonstrate Soviet hesitations. No: we are not dealing with the overthrow of a people's power abruptly driven to use violence or to accept the irretrievable: we are witnessing the incoherent activity, sometimes soft, sometimes harsh and hasty,

47

of a disunited government hampered by its internal differences, in its own ideology, which loses countenance before the attitude of its soldiers and discovers in amazement, but too late, the truth its servants had kept hidden from it. Intervention was made inevitable, not by a white terror in Budapest, but by the triumph of a certain policy in Moscow. We are expected to believe that it was necessary in the immediate situation and for universally valid reasons (that is to say, acceptable to every man of the Left). This is not true: men, embracing *a certain political perspective*, founded on an estimation *which is their own* of the international situation, have judged it preferable to refuse their chance to the socialist forces of the new Hungary, and to plunge that country into chaos. Events in Budapest were never judged in themselves: they were considered only in the light of the repercussions they might have in central Europe and, ultimately, on the two *blocs*.

Who, in fact, will be led to believe that the Soviets wanted, in Hungary, to defend Hungarian socialism? If they thought of doing that, what naïvety and what a defeat! What did they gain? Nothing. What did they lose? Everything. They caused a hatred to arise in hearts which is nowhere near to being extinguished, and which is of service to reaction. They have disqualified the Hungarian Party for ever, and forced it itself to deny itself by changing its name. They have succeeded in ruining the economy and when, for its reconstruction, the active co-operation of the whole people is required, they have put the masses against the government. They have installed in power a national Communist whose popularity might have been useful to them, but they have disqualified him in advance by forcing him to take on himself responsibility for the massacres. They have provoked a general strike of protest which proclaims the Red Army—the workers' army—the enemy of the workers of Hungary. They do not dare to have recourse to force openly in order to get the workers back into the factories; nevertheless they make an increasing number of arrests. If they leave, the leaders imposed on the Hungarian people will be swept away by the people's anger; if they stay, they condemn Kadar's only resource—democratization—to remain a dead letter. Caught in their own trap, they are stuck like birds on a limed twig in an occupation which I hope fills their troops with horror, justified

48

a little more each day by the evil it does and the resentment it engenders. Violence and oppression progressively move this martyred country away from the socialist camp; to keep it there, they have no longer any but one means: oppression and violence. Before this month of October, they were winning all along the line: they were issuing as victors from the cold war; reconciled with Tito, they were restoring the unity of the socialist camp, they were extending their influence in the Middle East and as far away as India. In the middle-class democracies, their cultural offensive was bearing fruit; the Twentieth Congress was taking the sting out of the enemy's propaganda. Today, Nehru condemns them; the Afro-Asian countries are hesitant, apprehensive; *Pravda* and *Borba* exchange abuse. The massacres of Budapest have reduced to nothing years of effort towards relaxing of tensions, co-existence, peace. In the West, Communists have never found themselves more isolated, never has their confusion been so great, never has the Right triumphed so noisily. All this could have been foreseen; in the dark days of November 2 and 3, when the radio announced the entry of Soviet reinforcements into Hungary, men of the Left, friends of the USSR and of the Communists, in France and everywhere else, weighed the conseqences of an attack and said to themselves, it's not possible, they won't do it.

They did it. But in the name of what? and what did they want to save? The answer is simple: those responsible for the intervention acted under the conviction that a world struggle was inevitable, they were inspired by the policy of *blocs* and the cold war.

When it came, what objectives it followed, what men carried it out, what is its significance for socialism: that is what I must now work out.

In our middle-class countries, we know the price that has had to be paid for 'primitive accumulation'; we do not forget the immense wastage of human lives, forced labour, wretchedness, rebellions, repression. It seems that the industrialization of the USSR cost less dear. What a terrible effort it demanded, nevertheless; what sweat, what blood: it was a timed race, in an under-developed, encircled, almost wholly agricultural country, which had to equip itself in spite of the economic blockade and

49

under the continual threat of armed aggression. No one will ever be able to say to what degree this 'besieged fortress' was able, without risking total destruction, to reduce the sufferings and the hardships of its inhabitants. What is certain is that the Communist leaders assumed entire responsibility for the régime in both its greatness and its defects. The liberal man of the middle classes pleads not guilty: he did not make the world, he like everyone else obeys the pitiless laws of the economy. But the Soviet revolutionaries, after several years of uncertainty, ended by realizing that socialism could not be separated from planning. Besides, the urgency of the dangers and the lack of culture of the masses forced the Russian government to declare in favour of an authoritarian system of planning. At once the leaders themselves became part of the Plan; the Plan assumed their faces, their voices, their hands. It became the real government. This alienation of the directorate from its undertaking could only accentuate the major contradiction of Soviet society: long-term interests of socialist construction were opposed to the immediate interests of the working class.

In a middle-class democracy, in fact, the proletariat is of itself, as Marx said, 'the decomposition of society in so far as it is a particular class'; in this negative situation, there is such an adaptation of its immediate reactions to its historical task that it is the masses who give the example of radicalism: their spontaneous claims have the effect of hastening the dissolution of capitalist society, while at the same time expressing the deep character of proletarians, 'the secret of their own existence'. Thus, the oppressed class has 'a universal character through its universal sufferings', and Marx was able to use the word 'must', which he borrowed from ethics, to characterize claims originating in immediate interests. In other words, the needs of the worker in a capitalist régime—his weariness, his hunger, for example—have in their nakedness an actual socialistic character. The result of exploitation, these needs cannot be asserted without calling exploitation in question; they cannot be appeased without diminishing profits and endangering capital. But, in Soviet Russia, the major worry of the leaders would be to realize material conditions which will allow of a solution of the problems created by the Revolution. Now, the spontaneous reactions of the masses retain their negative character in re-

50

lation to the general needs of the economy. In the period of post-revolutionary construction, at the moment when the socialist State wishes to provide the country with an industrial organization, there is a danger that everything may be compromised by the claim-making of the masses: the worker may reject intensive work, insist on a rise in wages, on clothes, on footgear, on homes. In short, his immediate interest leads him to claim the development of consumer industries in a society which will perish if it does not first devote itself to promoting heavy industry. Universal in a middle-class society, his claim becomes private in a post-revolutionary society. Moreover, his situation has not changed. It is true that he is no longer exploited, but 'the contradiction between his human *nature* and his vital existence' has not disappeared. Revolution, whatever it may be, does not work miracles; it inherits all the wretchedness produced by the former régime. Of course, this conflict is not confined to opposition between the Plan, the necessary condition of progress towards socialism, and the worker as the power of labour and a system of needs. It exists in each individual: for the worker wants both the realization of socialism and the satisfaction of his needs. In the name of the first, he will agree to curb the second; he can be asked to make serious sacrifices. But he develops a shifting in his objectives: in a capitalist régime, he aimed at the overturning of the middle class and the dictatorship of the proletariat through his concrete demands: distant targets gave *meaning* to immediate needs, immediate needs gave a *present* content to those targets. The worker was in tune with himself, and the leaders, organizing the movement of the masses all the while, could not escape from their control: they could lead them only where they wanaed to go. In time of post-revolutionary construction, the worker's socialism rests on a firm basis: socialization of the means of production.[27] He knows that sooner or later his efforts must be of benefit to the working class itself and, through it, to the whole people; work no longer strikes him as an inimical force, but as a concrete bond between the different social circles; a rational understanding of the situation and of its needs, unwillingness to compromise what has been achieved, fidelity to principles, to the target: all this predisposes him to curb his needs as far as he can, to regard his weariness

51

as a private event which concerns himself alone, whereas, while he was subject to middle-class exploitation, he saw it as the expression of the universal weariness of his class. It does not matter that his socialist targets no longer appear in the actual need which was the basis of his claims; even if he is willing to work more in order to free his sons from the compulsion of need, it is to his son's need, and not to his own, that he has tied the progress of industrialization. That is not to say that this divorce would have been so sharp if the October Revolution of 1917 had broken out in Germany or in Britain rather than in Russia; in those countries, which were already industrially equipped, the rhythm and the distribution of investment would have been different. But since the USSR had *before all else* to provide itself with capital equipment, of necessity it must be a very long time before the efforts and sacrifices of each individual had the *visible* effect of a rise in the standard of living. This real cleavage in the worker during the first phase of socialist construction is curiously underlined, in the new Poland, by the co-existence in certain undertakings of management committees and trade union councils elected by the same workers. Bourdet asked if there was not a danger that the work of one of these organizations would be duplicated by the other; the workers told him not: 'The committee of management, although emanating directly from us, is carried along by the general course of the economy; it represents us in our national universality as socialist workers, and on that account is in danger of under-estimating our concrete needs and our immediate interests; that is why the trade unions are necessary.' Thus socialist contradiction entails the need for a double representation of the same workers; the permanent opposition of the committee of management and the trade union simply serves to bring out into the light of day the conflict which each individual dimly lives. Perhaps this objectification makes it possible to get beyond the contradiction. In the USSR, in the heroic times of the first five-year plans, it would have been unthinkable. A mass of illiterate peasants snatched by the demands of concentration from the countryside swelled the proletariat from day to day; the civil war had decimated the working-class élite; these confused masses, with no political training, had no clear awareness of what they had to do or of their future; in them, the conflict between the universal and the particular existed only in an embryonic state; overworked, under-fed, they were above all characterized by their needs. At the level of the leaders, on the other hand, the contradiction was evident, but it seemed primarily a problem to be resolved within the framework of the Plan: human needs seemed to be a factor of the first importance but negative as tending to check production. It was human, it was prudent to make the largest concessions to them, taking into account the vital needs of the Soviet economy. In that first phase, the masses lost the power of proclaiming their own needs for themselves; it was the experts who determined what was proper to them. In the pre-revolutionary period, the trained personnel and the organization—however authoritarian they may have been—remained under the control of the working classes; after the Revolution, socialist experience escaped in part from this *human* control, it tended to substitute technical criteria for it. Compelled to *interpret* the objective contradictions of the economic movement, the leaders lost touch with the working-class condition; they were absorbed purely in knowledge of their objectivity and in the authoritative action which would resolve difficulties. The mass thus became a passive object, unaware of historical contradictions, while the leaders decided as to investment, norms of work, and standards of living by a real 'rational calculation'.

At about the same time, industrialization engenders a demographic upheaval which demands an increase in agricultural productivity. These changes lead to the sudden appearance of contradictions which put town workers against country workers. Compensation for the inadequacy of town workers' wages can be achieved only by the lowering and dictatorial stabilization of agricultural prices; country workers claim that manufactured products should bear the lowering of prices. The government sees itself under an obligation to effect collectivization of the fields by compulsion: large undertakings yield better and are more easily controlled. The working class unreservedly supports this policy of violence which serves the interests of urban concentrations. Besides, industrial workers consider nationalization of enterprises as the greatest victory of the proletariat; to them, collectivization of the fields appears to be a necessary consequence of the socialization of industry. The country folk,

53

on the contrary, even if they belong to a prosperous *kolkhoz*, continue to resist what they regard as expropriation.

In point of fact, both groups were subject to the absolute authority of the Plan: none the less, it is true that the arbitrary demands of the build-up worked out as a genuine class struggle between workers and peasants, so exacerbated as to become a civil war; deportations and executions did not suppress this struggle: beginning in 1930, the Soviet leaders, in the name of the proletariat, were compelled to exercise an iron dictatorship over a hostile peasantry.

Stalinism was born of this double contradiction. To begin with, the Plan created its own tools: it developed a bureaucracy of experts, technicians, and administrators as rationalization, in capitalist countries, has developed the 'tertiary' class.[28] It is absurd to assert that this bureaucracy *exploits* the proletariat and that it is a *class*, for in that case these words no longer have any meaning. Neither is it true to say that its sole care is the defence of its own interests. Its members are much too well paid, but they use themselves up on the job; they put in longer hours at work than do the workers. Born of the Plan, their privileges are justified by the Plan: their personal ambition is not distinguishable from their devotion to socialism conceived as abstract planning: that is to say, in the end, as continuous increase in production. This total alienation allows them to regard themselves as organs of the universal to the extent that the Plan has to be established by their care. The claims of the masses, on the contrary, even if they take account of them, are for them special contingencies of a strictly negative character. And, in actual fact, their position is in itself contradictory, for it is true that they represent the universal in so far as they want to carry the whole country along to the building up of socialism, and it is also true that they represent a simple *particularism* to the extent that their function has cut them off from the Russian people and from its concrete life. Between these 'organizers' and the masses, the Party claims to play the part of a mediator. As a matter of fact, it continually corrects the bureaucracy; by unceasing importunities, by modifications, by 'purges', it keeps it on the alert and prevents it from setting itself up on its own account; but the Party is, in itself, the political expression of planning; creator of myths, specialized in propaganda, it controls, agitates, exhorts the masses. It can unite them at one moment in a unanimous movement, but it does not reflect, any more than do the trade unions, their immediate interests, their claims, or the currents which stir them. The working classes close in on themselves and their real life falls into a kind of clandestinity: this remoteness engenders mutual distrust. Much later the leaders ask themselves (they were putting the question to themselves in 1954, when I was in Moscow) how to interest the masses *as such* in production; but problems are not formulated except when means are available to solve them. Today the extraordinary advances in the Soviet economy make it possible to envisage real solutions: in a capitalist régime, the revolutionary movement is distinguished by the deep unity of its distant objectives and its immediate targets, but this unity defines it as negativity. At a certain stage in socialization, the development of the Soviet economy made it easier to unify the people's objectives in a positive process of construction. But in the period which followed the Revolution, pre-revolutionary unity gave place to an insuperable contradiction. At that time it became necessary to create a working-class élite for whom growth in production would be translated immediately into a material change for the better, and who would find its most immediate interest in realizing and going beyond the Plan. This joining of immediate well-being to the socialist build-up was completely artificial: it was brought about by authority and, for some, by taking up available plus-value. These 'heroes of labour' are cited everywhere as an example, but the example is false: their small number is the very condition of their prosperity. At the same time, their existence alone is enough, sometimes without the knowledge of the masses, to bring about a general increase in norms. The necessities of socialization incline the leaders to under-estimate the revolutionary strength of the proletariat; they work on it from outside by propaganda, by disguised compulsion, by emulation, and in any event they prefer to the proletariat Stakhanovites who, like themselves, are born of the Plan and like themselves alienated to increase of production. On their side, the working-class masses approve of the régime, but they have no confidence in the bureaucracy. Between an alienated bureaucracy and a crushed peasantry, undoubtedly the workers in industry alone retain a measure of

55

independence and even—within well defined limits—a certain right to criticize. It is not the less true that they feel themselves ruled from outside. The proletariat is no longer the subject of history, it is not yet the concrete target of socialization: it feels itself the *principal object* of administrative solicitude and the *essential means* of building up socialism. For that precise reason, socialism remains its class 'duty' and ceases to be its reality. However, the bureaucracy works unceasingly on itself and pursues its unification without slackening. The contradictions of socialism, and the conflict of proletariat and peasant in particular, compel the leaders to cut their corners, continually to diverge, to correct earlier deviations. The existence of a Rightish fraction and a Leftish fraction at the heart of the administration would disseminate the gravest dangers to planning; from what may be only a tactical retreat or a provisional hardening, *one* policy will appear to be triumphing: that is to say, one team and one programme. In point of fact, the Plan is only a hypothesis which is subject continuously to the test of experience and which it must be possible to correct without bias, as a function of actual experience. The urgency of correction implies total agreement among the organizers; this agreement alone will prevent a temporary deviation from being adopted for its own sake, from changing the *trend*; it alone will make possible the cancellation of all harmful measures, even one that has just been stopped; it alone makes the leaders conform constantly to objectivity. On the other hand, there is no doubt about the threats from abroad; in spite of which the dumb, hostile mass of country folk refuses to rally; compulsion therefore has to be increased. Now, a dictatorial group must first of all impose dictatorship on itself. Thus, external danger and internal resistance exact indissoluble unity from the leaders. Without deep roots, without real support, the group of 'organizers' can maintain its authority and ensure national security only if it first of all works out *from the inside*, by itself and through itself, its own security; events oblige it to push its own integration to the limit. But the limit is never reached, for the biological and mental unity of the individual supplies the best image of it. From this, this strange contradiction results: each individual becomes suspect in the eyes of all, and even in his own eyes, through this single reason that his

56

unity puts a check on absolute assimilation; but *only* one individual is capable of becoming the example, the agent, and the ideal expression of a social process of unification. At the very moment each individual feels himself inessential in relation to the group taken as an entity, this entity must remain a simple operative symbol, or the multiplicity of men must go beyond itself and re-assemble in a unity consecrated to an essential individuality. Thus the cult of personality is above everything the cult of social unity in one person. And Stalin's function was not to represent the indissolubility of the group, but *to be* that very indissolubility, and to forge it as a whole. No one should be astonished to see this idolatry spring up in a régime which denounces and rejects middle-class individualism, for it is simply the product of this rejection. Each middle-class person resembles all the others in this: that he insists on his own difference and on the value of his own personality; these barbarous assertions balance one another; the apparent reciprocity of relations universalizes them; the middle-class man respects in himself, and claims to respect in others, the absolute dignity of the human individual. Beyond that, this cult falls into abstraction. Since each is sacred, none is so. Under cover of this respect, realist appreciation of one's self and of others will depend on the particular content of this universal form: abilities, actions, character. These material elements may form the object of a hierarchy, but not of a cult: no one of them is valued *a priori*. Thus individualism excludes all possibilities of idolatry. The function of the leading lady, the star, the 'great man', indispensable properties of middle-class ceremonies, is most certainly not to demonstrate the absolute superiority of the few over the majority; in the eyes of each of the rest they embody his own possibilities. Loaded with honours, at the summit of glory and power, by their very existence they do more than the cleverest propaganda: contrary to all truth, their existence persuades the rest that the highest dignities are accessible to the humblest citizen. The function—as abstract power—is identified with the personality as pure form; this entity is the object of a cult, it is sacred; the *real* qualities of the individual are beside the point. Every moderately pretty girl respects the star in Brigitte Bardot, but is quite sure that this actress's qualities cannot entirely justify her lofty position; there is such a displacement

57

between the concrete individuality and what I shall call the 'personality-function' that only by chance does the first slip into the second. Now chance *is nothing*; so that every celebrated woman performer reflects back to all the women of France their own possibilities of becoming consecrated.[29]

In subordinating his person to the group, the Soviet man avoids the preposterous vices of middle-class personalization. But, at the same time, the continuously more imperative need to maintain and strengthen unity causes his individual reality to fall into clandestinity; in spite of the Constitution, he is deprived of status and remains a simple factor of multiplicity, the possible source of disunity and the object of a latent distrust. Struggles, however terrible they may be, remain in the field of objectivity: solutions, projects are in opposition to one another, but ambition, self-assertion remain implicit, they never appear in broad daylight; the Plan covers them over and absorbs them. For lack of manifestation, individual wills can neither recognize nor balance one another in a system which should be a complete guarantee against all overgrowth of the cult of personality. In point of fact, Stalin does not at first appear as an individual superior to the rest but at bottom like everyone else; he represents not the dignity of the individual, but social integration pushed to the limit. This indissolubility—which *happens* to be that of the individual—makes of him the only possible agent of unification, for unity alone can unify multiplicity. He is identified with the coercive action which the group exerts on its members; he will carry out the sentence passed by the bureaucracy on itself; he takes up and interiorizes the diffused distrust of the revolutionary collectivity. In the name of all, he will distrust each one; but the group will not distrust him. Placed at the heart of the bureaucracy, he might have represented only plurality and division; placed above it, he reflects back to it the impossible collective unity; the right hand of Stalin does not distrust his left hand, nor his left ear his right ear. Stalin cannot become the spy of Stalin nor cease to be in agreement with himself. The group cannot continue to exist without confidence; it is not enough to say that it trusts Stalin, rather it takes its own confidence from the confidence Stalin has in himself. No one *enjoys* that confidence except Stalin in person; but each one knows that up there, in Stalin, the bureaucratic collectivity exists under a form of superior integration, and that it is brought together. So each member of the bureaucracy, far from seeing in Stalin an exaltation of the human individual, discovers in this concentration of collectivity the radical negative of his own individuality, to the gain of unity. The ascending movement which goes from the group to Stalin is thus distinguished by the total destruction of individuality.

On the other hand, there is a descending movement: Stalin can solve the problem of integration only by pushing the social hierarchy to the limit. From top to bottom of the ladder, directly or indirectly, those responsible hold their power from him. So the *person* is seen to be reborn. But this person has nothing in common with the middle-class individual: he does not owe his existence to a universal status, but to the unique person whom the necessities of integration place above the group. His reality, always subject to recall, comes to him from his very functions; in his relations with his equals, it remains a factor of multiplicity, therefore an object of distrust; for his subordinates, on the other hand, it is a hypostasis of Stalin, therefore a factor of unification and an object of worship. At all levels of the hierarchy, we find the same contradiction. Biological and mental autonomy appears as an element of plurality and as a symbol of integration; the same individual poses as a synthetic force before his subordinates and denies his living reality in his relations with those above him. In any event, what lays the foundations of the Soviet person and at the same time destroys him is the impossible unity of the group. Stalin alone is pure unity: he is the act. It is not his private qualities which are adored in him; still less is it some 'charismatic' power or other, such as that the Nazis recognized in Hitler. There is nothing mystical about his cult: it applies to a real unity in so far as it is the power of unification. It is besides inseparable from terror: Stalin embodying the collective distrust can reach the end of multiplicity only by trying to reduce it. The negative opposite of hierarchical build-up is the revolving terror which the bureaucracy exercises on itself through Stalin's hands and which is translated into 'purges' and deportations.

'Socialism in one country', or Stalinism, does not form a deviation from socialism: it is the roundabout way imposed on him by circumstances. The rhythm and the evolution of this

59

defensive construction are not determined only by consideration of Soviet resources and needs, but also by the relations of the USSR with the capitalist world; in short, by circumstances external to socialization which compel him unceasingly to compromise with his principles. The contradictions of this first phase give rise to a class conflict between workers and peasants and cut across the leaders of the working masses; an authoritarian and bureaucratic system is set up in which everything is sacrificed to productivity. This system reflects its contradictions in its ideological superstructures: it claims Marxism-Leninism as its authority, but this cover ill dissembles a double judgement of value about man and above socialism. On one side, propaganda and rosy tales of 'socialist realism' call a sufficiently nauseous optimism to witness: in a socialist country, everything is fine, there is no conflict between the forces of the past and those which are building the future; these must of necessity triumph. Failures, sorrow, death—all are taken up and saved by the movement of history. For some time, it may even seem expedient to tell tales with no conflicts. Anyway, the positive hero knows nothing of internal difficulties and contradictions; for his part, he contributes, unfailingly and without mistakes, to the building up of socialism, his model is the young Stakhanovite; a soldier, he knows nothing of fear. These industrial and military sheepfolds call Marxism to witness: they show us the happiness of a society without class.

On the other hand, the exercise of dictatorship and the internal contradictions of bureaucracy necessarily engender a pessimism which dare not mention its name: since government is conducted by force, men must therefore be bad. These heroes of labour, these grand, devoted officials, these Party militants, so upright, so pure—a breath of wind can extinguish their most glowing virtues: they are counter-revolutionaries, spies, agents of capitalism. Habits of integrity, uprightness, thirty years of faithful service to the CP—nothing can defend them against temptation. And if they diverge from the line, it is soon discovered that they were guilty *from birth*. The great actions which brought them so many honours and so many encomiums were, it is suddenly discovered, heinous crimes: it is necessary to be prepared to revoke all judgements, to despise a man who has been cracked up to the skies without feeling any surprise at having been deceived for so long. In this dim and muddled world, today's truth must be asserted so much the more strongly the more the chances are of its being tomorrow's error. The State, far from withering away, must grow stronger: its withering away will come when an authoritarian upbringing has interiorized in each man the constraints it exercises: it will be made useless not by the emancipation of men, but by their self-domestication and their inward conditioning. It will not disappear, it will be transplanted into their hearts. It is this suspicion of man which is expressed in Stalin's famous 'theoretical mistake': the struggle between the classes is intensified during the period of socialist construction. It has been alleged that, cynically, he wanted to justify his 'practice'. Why? It is the practice, here, which engenders its correct theory. Besides, this pessimism is to be found in foreign politics. The USSR does not want war, but sees it coming: with good reason, since Hitler's armies invaded the country in 1941. But these completely valid fears entail a glaring simplification of the problems. The capitalist world, out of reach, badly understood, becomes a purely destructive force which mercilessly pursues the extermination of the Soviet people and the liquidation of the arms of socialism: its contradictions, the conflicts which they may bring about, the forces for peace which in the West are opposed to the forces of war are still mentioned. They are mentioned, but no one believes in them, above all since the failure of the *Front Populaire*: its only sure policy, in the state of isolation in which socialist Russia finds itself, is to arm itself, to arm itself ceaselessly *as if war were coming tomorrow*. Thus external and internal policy must be continually decided in the light of the risks of catastrophe, never in sympathy with the chances of peace. So long as it has not caught up with the nations of the West, the USSR must remain faithful to the pessimistic principle: *Si vis pacem, para bellum*, which might be rendered the worst is always certain.

Must socialism be called that bloody monster which itself tears itself to pieces? I answer candidly: yes. That was socialism even in its primitive phase; there has been no other, except perhaps in Plato's heaven, and it must be desired as it is or not desired at all. The failure of the USSR came, in 1945, from its victory: at Yalta it secured a zone of influence which, for the first time, put it in the position of exercising supremacy over a

61

group of foreign nations. Up to then, obsessed by fear of encirclement, this enormous continental power, shut in on itself, encysted, had sought safety only in increased armaments and in the tightening of its internal links; it had never felt the need nor found the occasion to provide itself with such agencies as would have allowed it to extend its influence outside: it had won even the war on its own soil by a kind of contraction. It emerged from its solitude full of distrust, and Stalin dreaded that decisive test for his soldiers: contact with the West.[30] Russia required the friendship of these enforced but necessary allies, but they inspired Russia only with distrust. Some of them were yesterday's enemies; most of them presented a picture of its own old structure: many peasants, few workers; in Rumania, in Hungary, not a Communist. Besides, Russia placed hardly any value on the workers, Communist or not, outside its own homeland. During the 1920s, the Russians had desired world revolution too ardently not to have a feeling of rancour against the European proletariats which had not made it. To begin with, the slope had only a military interest; the Red Army undertook to bring about revolution everywhere: there was no question, then, of exporting socialism but of creating people's governments which, in defending the USSR, defended themselves; everywhere coalition governments were set up in which the Communists, often in a minority, had only a hidden influence.

The Marshall Plan changed everything. This war manoeuvre uncovered a disquieting truth: the USA could come immediately to the help of these poor or ruined countries, the USSR had not yet got the means of equipping them; the political solidarity which had, with great difficulty, just been established would not weigh heavily against the economic solidarity offered by the West; already the hesitations of Czechoslovakia indicated how fragile the system was. Unable to take up the challenge, the Soviet government had to give up its allies or hold them by force. It chose to tighten its hold, to ensure Communist dictatorship everywhere, and to launch all the 'satellites' into the building of socialism.

It was quite right: at the time, the balance of forces was unfavourable to the USSR; the return of the satellites to a capitalist régime would have represented for the Soviet government the renewal and the augmentation of encirclement. Before

62

1939, central Europe was destroying itself; in each country, ethnic minorities, in endless ferment, represented a permanent risk of separatism and civil war; each was set against all the others by conflicting interests, rivalries, old hatreds. Paralysed by these dissensions, this large region, full of still unexploited riches, was above all the passive stake in the struggle of German imperialism against that of the Western democracies. The USSR might be threatened across it but not by it. After 1945, the situation was entirely changed. The crushing of Germany had created a void in Europe. With their own hands, the Soviets had raised up the small nations again. The war had put a brake on ethnic and national rivalries; in each country, a strong power had carried true unity into effect. If they escaped from Russian control, the people's democracies, fed, equipped with tools, armed by the United States, would become, on the threshold of Russia, the enemy's advanced frontiers. This direct and active threat would make the position of the Soviet Union still more difficult than it had been in the time of Hitler's Germany. No one seriously contemplated the possibility that they could remain neutral. Neutrality depends on historical conjuncture: today, the balance of forces tends towards equilibrium; it is thus no longer nonsensical that certain nations, in certain circumstances, lay claim to a neutral status guaranteed by all the powers. Nor that peoples call for the end of the cold war and of *blocs*. In 1948, the danger came from want of balance: it was not in the power of any State to spare itself the barren and grievous effort which should one day lead to the re-establishment of equality of military potential. The Red Army was in the heart of Europe, in Berlin; America had partially disarmed, but from day to day was adding to its stock of atomic weapons; the USA dreaded a conventional war which would carry Russian soldiers to the shores of the Atlantic; the USSR was afraid of perishing in the course of a new war, with unforeseeable developments, led by technicians, far away, with arms of which the West had made sure of the actual monopoly. This reciprocity of terror cut the world in two: it was not possible to cling to one of the fields of force without being caught up by the other.

In this conjuncture, the Marshall Plan seemed to be a provocation: under its pacific externals, it was the beginning of a policy of 'pressing back'. Since the Soviets had not yet got the means of fighting this economic penetration on its own ground, they were reduced to opposing it by force. They were losing on all counts: the USSR had allowed its weakness to be seen; even in the people's democracies, clever propaganda accused it of answering the disinterested offer of the United States by acts of force and of egoistically depriving the under-developed countries of help which was indispensable to them. The Russian leaders had seen the pitfall and did not hesitate to accept their responsibilities. In principle, their policy was right: by the pressure they brought to bear on their allies, they were saving peace and the building up of socialism in the USSR; *they were also making it possible to preserve the chances of socialization in central Europe.*

On condition that this socialization was undertaken *in the interests* of the small nations, taking into account their situation, their needs, and their resources, their social structures, their internal resistances, it was necessary and possible to save them from the terrible experiences of the Soviet Union. Now that is exactly what the Russian leaders were not willing to understand. Justifiably proud of their tragic and imposing history, did they really believe that all other nations had to do was to reproduce it automatically? Led astray by superficial analogies, had they no perception of differences which jumped to the eye? Moreover, it is obvious that the Soviets, in spite of their wonderful doggedness of purpose, could never have achieved 'socialism in one country' without the immense natural riches of Russia.[31] Central Europe most certainly does not lack resources, but they are unequally distributed between the nations. A socialist build-up necessitated the close union of all the people's democracies, and the drawing up in common of plans of production. That is what Nagy very clearly explained, in 1953, in his speech to Parliament: 'Nothing', he said, 'justifies exaggerated industrialization: and this effort to bring about national self-sufficiency in industry, above all if we have not at our disposal the necessary resources in raw materials, constitutes a renunciation of the advantageous possibilities resulting from a more intense international exchange of goods, and above all of economic collaboration with the USSR, the people's democracies, and the people's China. The accent must be put on light and food industries

64

while considerably reducing the rhythm of development of heavy industry.' By that he did not, as some believed, mean to cry down the priority of heavy industry, any more than the present breakdown of the economies of Hungary and Poland necessarily calls this principle in question. What the Soviets call 'the priority growth in the production of the means of production' is a necessity which is to be found also in capitalist economy since technical progress is reduced, in the last analysis, to the increasing preponderance of the machine in the manufacture of products. Only this necessity—except in the case of certain particularly favoured powers—has as its main effect, in the West, reinforcement of the links of dependence between nations and of accelerating the establishment of cartels, combines, and international pools. Everything is governed, to be sure, by the search for profit, but, in the present phase of industrial development, unification of complementary economies is everywhere indispensable, whatever the régime may be. And Nagy had no wish to say anything else: as he saw it, the priority of heavy industry could assert itself only within an organic whole in which the resources of soil and subsoil sustained and satisfied the demands of industrialization. One of his immediate colleagues was even more explicit: 'We have made a mistake because we have interpreted badly the policy of socialist industrialization.' The development of light industries as it was attempted by the Nagy government from 1953–1955 did not mean abandonment of the 'Marxist-Leninist' thesis: it merely put the accent on the impossibility *in Hungary* of carrying 'socialism in one country' into effect. The astounding folly of Stalin and the Stalinists was to believe in pre-established harmony, or to allow this harmony to be believed in: how explain, in fact, except by recourse to Providence, that each of the people's democracies should find itself at the same time the complex product of universal history and an economic organism concealing within itself all, or nearly all, the conditions for its own autonomy? By what aberration did it come to be believed that each of them had the duty to push industrialization to the limit in order to establish its sovereignty on a genuine self-sufficiency? And who, conequently, could imagine that the sweat and blood of the workers would impregnate the land and create coal or iron in the very places where these minerals did not exist?

To begin with, no one supported this idiotic doctrine: as early as 1945, on the contrary, certain central European states put forward the idea of an economic federation. It can be guessed that Stalin did not regard this idea with favour. It seems, nevertheless, that he was not altogether opposed to it; Tito had some strange conversations with him on this subject. As a matter of fact, the most strenuous resistance came from the small Balkan powers, always jealous of their autonomy; but it goes without saying that the federation—with or without them—would have been effected if only the Kremlin had decided on it. In any event, the Marshall provocation destroyed at one blow the weak chances of federalism. The rank obstinacy of distrust triumphed. It was not enough to snatch these states from the hold of the West; it was necessary to isolate them, to divide in order to rule. 'Socialism in one country' had been the doctrine and the gigantic undertaking of a nation cut off from the world. To cut each of the people's democracies off from the encompassing world, each one of them was given as its creed and its task 'socialism in one country'. Stalinism did not cease to exploit the political enmities of the satellites; in order to mask them, at least in certain sectors, where their economies could have become complementary, they were obliged to provide themselves artificially with homologous economies. With the help of the USSR—experts, markets, material aid in case of urgency—each threw itself into super-industrialization, and into accelerated collectivization in the agricultural sector. This sudden madness ought to have had a different effect: it was certainly assumed that these peoples, absorbed in an immense labour of construction, would forget Marshall and his works; socialization *à la Russe* was their proud reply to the offers from abroad: we need no one, we are working to be sufficient to ourselves. The USSR was their guide, philosopher, and friend; it was guiding its younger sisters towards plenty: its solicitude would obliterate remembrance of the feebleness of its material aid. In each of the people's democracies, the leaders fell in with the situation: Soviet dictatorship had to be masked by exalting excessive patriotism; the wonderful effort of the people who were winning independence by the sweat of their brows was insisted on. Their leaders wanted to give them tangible symbols of their victories: Rakosi had an underground constructed in Budapest

66

against the advice of experts; he built Stalinvaros, an extra-ordinary dead city, an immense building site where nobody worked. Polish Stalinists wanted to endow that country with a motor vehicle industry. In short, attempts were made to base a new nationalism on the greatness of 'realizations'. Entirely cut off from its neighbours, each country adopted the retractile structure of Soviet society; masked its state of bondage and its wretchedness by building a gigantic piece of camouflage.

The target was reached quickly: the governments sent one another telegrams; they were able to exchange duty visits with one another. The nations were able to exchange delegations, but the real relations of Prague and Warsaw, of Belgrade and Budapest necessarily passed through Moscow. This once again is the principle of the Stalinist hierarchy: subordinates com-municate with one another only through the instrumentality of their superior. That was Stalin's fundamental mistake: rather than attach its allies to itself by a real and positive solidarity; the USSR preferred to create abortions which could not con-tinue to exist without it.

At the very moment when nationalism was being exalted, Stalinist distrust laid itself out to humiliate it. The impassable chasm which separated these prefabricated revolutions from the October Revolution does not in fact appear to have occurred to anyone. The October Revolution was autochthonous. What-ever may have been its later contradictions and the hierarchical form of the society they engendered, it came from below; it was carried through by the masses, at least in the beginning. For the people's democracies, on the contrary, socialism was an imported commodity; revolution was made from above; its leaders had been imposed on them by the Red Army, and many of them had come back from Moscow. The only government which enjoyed the confidence of the people, that of Tito, drew from the support of the masses the strength to oppose the de-mands of the USSR. The result is known: everywhere else, Stalinist distrust, strengthened, exacted the liquidation of 'national Communists'. Now, these were the only ones who had fought in the Resistance, the only ones who retained some personal influence over the workers. The men who remained, however devoted they may have been to socialism, owed their power only to the support of the foreigner. I have described how the Soviet bureaucracy had cut itself off from the masses. But I have shown also that this cutting off was the consequence of inevitable contradictions and extreme dangers. In the people's democracies, the brutal dissolution of the 'fronts' and the Stalinization of the Communist Parties carried this cutting off into effect *in advance* and threw discredit on the new policy when there had been no time to prepare it. These governments, born of the cold war, judged it well to exalt nationalism in words when their very existence humiliated it; they did not understand that they were forging an army which would sooner or later turn on them. Rakosi pushed his mental blindness still further; a Jew, surrounded by Jews, he was not afraid to arouse the anti-Semitism of the Hungarians by a violent anti-Zionist campaign.

Everything flowed away into abstraction: Merleau-Ponty is right in referring in this connexion to the failure of 'voluntary' planning which ends up in 'unreal' projects. But he is wrong to extend this censure to the plans made for the USSR by Soviet experts, the best informed on the demands and possibilities of their national economy. The results anticipated were certainly not always attained, but the projects, however authoritarian and 'voluntary' they may have been, remained valid within a certain margin of error, or at least amenable to correction, in so far as they were *national*. In the people's democracies, the plans, drawn up by Russian experts, took no account of the actual conditions of production; once they were completed, no one could call them in question. Now these plans were only dreams: of course they exacted *too much* and *too quickly*, but above all they asked for something else. Something that it was impossible to give. They imposed on the country an artificial economy which the real economy could not support. In order to keep up by force these alien structures, the national revenue was increasingly depleted from one day to the next. In Hungary, carrying out the Plan between 1951 and 1953, the proportion of investment in heavy industry (added to consumption by State organizations, and by the administrative apparatus) never stopped growing: fixed at first at 28 per cent, two years later it was swallowing half the revenue. Better: when Soviet demands changed, a partial redistribution of investment was arranged to satisfy them, without any reconsideration of the Plan as a whole; as a result, certain sectors suddenly went sickly and others grew to excess; cankers ate into the economy.

Everyone is aware of the consequences: everywhere, the hostility of the country folk wrecked the co-operatives; the governments were not sure enough of their troops to have recourse to force. The visible presence of the occupier poisoned everything: would Hungarian soldiers have fired on Hungarian peasants in order to compel them to follow directives from a foreigner? Could recourse be had to Russian troops without worsening the situation? The real power of the dictators was less solid than it had at first appeared to be: they could hang bureaucrats, but they could not rally the peasants nor could they keep the workers in their place of employment. Besides, the farmers knew the tragic history of Soviet collectivization: it will be appreciated that before the war the middle-class and Fascist press had complacently given them this information; they did not try to oppose by force the setting up of co-operatives, but their passive resistance ended by ruining the system. When it did not go down, the standard of living remained stationary; in numbers of industrial sectors, despite the immense effort imposed on the workers, productivity never reached pre-war levels. The targets fixed under the Plan were reached only on paper. Each of the people's democracies was twofold: there was the mirage society and the real society. The mirage society was the USSR writ small: a bureaucracy drunk on statistics guided the working-class masses towards socialism with an iron hand; from top to bottom, the hierarchical order was a little compressed but sustained individuals. The real society was the spinning of an economy and a bureaucracy which had together fallen into a panic and then into the void, and then, at the level of the masses, there was an extraordinary mixture of compulsion and anarchy.[32] The system continued because no one knew the whole truth: workers and technicians saw in their part of the whole the seriousness of the mistakes made but could not imagine that the same situation could be true in all other sectors. The leaders did not realize the extent of the disasters: they were lied to, they lied to Stalin. Stalin and the political bureau were stubborn in error: the attribute of pessimism was confirmed by its effects. After the Marshall operation, the Soviet leaders judged war to be more likely than peace.

The logical consequence of this assessment was rearmament; it was also the policy of *blocs*. In this perspective, which bolstered mistrust, it was natural to treat as suspects those strange allies who had been eager in 1948 to lend an ear to the over beautiful sirens of the Atlantic. The USSR is said to have *colonized* the satellite countries: that is false. Colonization is a well-defined economic system whose characteristics are not to be found here: where have colonizers been seen to force the colonized to industrialize themselves? The mother country exports finished products in order to import raw materials or food products; now, between the USSR and the people's democracies the nature of their exchanges is to a high degree variable: Russia may buy mineral products and pay for them with cereals (Polish coal against Soviet wheat); it may develop (in Czechoslovakia and even in Hungary) industries complementary to its own: in that case, it may perhaps deliver raw materials against its imports, that is to say play the part of the under-developed country.[33] In other instances, the exchange turns on manufactured objects. Undoubtedly, it will be said; but there is *exploitation*. All the same, that is not true. Or, at least, it is not the essential point. Certainly the Soviet leaders have always sought to work out agreements which would be advantageous to them. They have put their hands without a by-your-leave on Hungarian uranium. When they created mixed societies, they organized them so that the assessment of contributions would assure a supplementary margin of profit to Russia; nor is there any doubt that they bought Polish coal below its market price. But, there also, there has been exaggeration, or the question has been wrongly stated: the reproach levelled at the Russians by many Communists in the people's democracies was not that they bought below world prices (although that may have happened) but, entirely to the contrary, that they take world prices as the basis of their calculations with the immediate result that they are unfair to the under-developed nation. In short, they reproach these socialists for acting *like capitalists*, and not for giving themselves up to I know not what super-exploitation which would make even capitalists blush. In any event, that is not what has ruined the economies of the satellites; and it should not be forgotten that this partial exploitation is counter-balanced in case of urgency by material

70

aid. No, the USSR has not colonized nor systematically exploited the people's democracies. What is true is that it has *oppressed* them for eight years. It could have tried to win their friendship, and deliberately, through pessimism and contempt, it has preferred coercion; this great lonely country has not known how to crack its shell of routine and suspicion, nor has it wished to do so, in order to adapt itself to its new situation and to assume the leadership of central Europe. I have said suspicion pays: oppressed, ruined, treated as suspects, these allies have become less and less safe. Force is its own evidence; in 1948 one would bet on it; today it alone guarantees the fidelity of Hungary to the Russians.

From the time of Stalin, however, the sore places remained covered over. No one can doubt that events in Poland and in Hungary have been a direct effect of what is called here de-Stalinization. De-Stalinization, democratization—whatever name is given to it—this extraordinary upheaval does not come from pressure by the masses. Since its birth, the Stalinist régime has not ceased to destroy itself to the exact extent that, in conformity with his function, Stalin constructed a society completely different from that which had produced him. In Stalin's last years, Stalinism forged all the tools of its liquidation; it was a relic, deeply at variance with the real structure of the new society. The USSR had acquired an enormous military potential: the Red Army was strong enough to reach the Atlantic in forty-eight hours; the armament industry was making atomic bombs. It was not certain, in a world conflict, that the Russians would win, but it was apparent already that they could not be attacked without putting the human race on the brink of total disappearance. In the same time—and *in spite of* Stalin's systematic suspicion—a great Communist power had just been born which had made its own revolution, without help, and which—unlike the people's democracies—had from the begining, indissolubly united the demands of socialist construction with those of the national interest:[34] Mao's China saved the USSR from encirclement. It is too little to declare, as has been done, that these new conditions make possible a policy of relaxation: they demand it. Vulnerable, alone, and hemmed in, the USSR could appear violent without ceasing to assert its will to peace: the balance of forces was unfavourable to it. The

71

intransigence of its diplomacy and, if I may say so, its aggressiveness remained defensive; its relative inferiority put it under the necessity of refusing—at least in appearance—all concessions. This negative attitude corresponded perfectly to the Stalinist 'retraction'. But when Stalin announced that Soviet industry was making atomic missiles, when Mao proclaimed the Chinese Republic, this 'retractile' attitude became more and more dangerous: the balance of forces tending to become equal, Stalinist aggressiveness, in spite of itself, changed its meaning and became objectively offensive. The war in Korea was the test: it is clear that the USSR was not responsible and that these local operations represent an episode in the conflict otherwise serious which put the people's China over against the America of MacArthur and of the 'China lobby'.[35] But the American government judged otherwise. We know how the public was worked up by press campaigns and how anti-Sovietism was exacerbated. It remains that the 'awakening' of the USA, the hardening of its policy, McCarthyism, and the decision to re-arm Germany bore witness to sudden panic: the USSR was becoming strong enough to reveal its imperialism; in the USA, the clique of war-mongers took on a growing importance. The Kremlin had to resign itself to war or take up an attitude more consistent with its new and terrible power. At the same moment, besides, the triumph of the Chinese Communists drew the USSR out of its solitude, but, on the other hand, called on it to establish, *with one country at least*, true socialist relations. There could be no question of subjecting and enfeoffing a nation of six hundred million inhabitants; nevertheless, China was under-developed. Between the two economies the disparity was such that there was a risk of drawing the Soviets into the slippery slope of semi-colonialism; it was necessary to choose between exploitation which, however discreet, the Chinese economy would not have tolerated, and the truly socialist practice of disinterested help. Only this policy of giving allowed the USSR to preserve its hegemony in the socialist world. Still, it must be added that this hegemony, in China, could not but remain very limited; the Soviet leaders were not unaware of this: it was through China, and through it alone, that they could exert their influence on the Asiatic world; but the prestige of the Chinese Republic rested inseparably on its independence

72

and on its sovereignty. Beginning in 1949, the USSR found itself compelled, for the first time, to base its relations with a foreign nation on confidence and generosity.[36]

Meanwhile, the structure of Soviet society continued to change. Economic blockade was no longer to be feared: the USSR had become the second industrial power in the world. The priority accorded to heavy industry and armaments had put a brake on the raising of the standard of living, but had not stopped it. This raising mitigated the basic contradiction between the demands of industrialization and the needs of the workers. The standard of culture had risen considerably: educated, aware, the young workers had nothing in common with the illiterate masses of 1926; they could gauge and give their support to rational and clearly explained planning; on the other hand, it was with difficulty that they put up with the authoritarianism of the little Stalins in factory or workshop; with more difficulty still did they put up with a Stakhanovite élite whose interests were opposed to their own. The new generation of country workers knew nothing of the pre-war massacres and deportations; they began, on the contrary, to feel the benefits of motorization: that is what brought them, little by little, into closer harmony with the régime. At the head of factories and of state undertakings, a generation of technicians, tough and ambitious but solidly moulded, rediscovered *in work* free relations with peasants and workers. There has been talk of 'technocracy': it is absurd. But there is no doubt that the second phase of socialist construction is distinguished by the growing importance of technique, and that specialists are protected in it and valued according to their functions. This new importance in direct connexion with productivity tends to protect them from Stalinism: their dedication comes from their abilities; that is what protects them against the risks of disgrace, and is the basis in each one of them of his awareness that he is something in himself.

Nevertheless, at the top, dictatorship grew desperate; terror fell into a panic, spun more and more quickly, massacred everything. The isolation of the Party was emphasized; from top to bottom of the social ladder, an incompetent bureaucracy doubled the new technical personnel. This bureaucracy had had its heroic hour: when technical personnel was lacking, it had taught itself everything, rapidly provided itself with culture and the technical knowledge that allowed it, somehow or other, to direct industrialization. Stalin was the model for these great workers: he read everything, knew everything, gave his decision on everything; he found the time to have all films projected before him, to judge all novels, all musical compositions; the needs of his varied functions had obliged him to acquire what one might call, with a mixture of disapproval and admiration, universal incompetence. But, to the precise extent that these bureaucrats *took the place* of experts and specialists, to the extent that they provided the solder between the ignorant Russia of the Tsars and the industrialized USSR, they were digging their own grave; higher education, created and developed through their care, continually produced more numerous technicians whose rôle was, rightly, to eliminate them. They remained in place, nevertheless, these Stalinists who owed everything to Stalin: the bureaucracy, in alliance with the Party, distrusted the new-comers and believed itself to be the sole trustee of the revolutionary impulse: that meant, above all, that it considered itself alone qualified to devise the plans and to ensure their carrying out. Thus, in the last years of Stalin, the movement of socialization engendered a hidden contradiction, still masked by dictatorship but bound to break through sooner or later: in producing its new technical personnel, it placed them over against the old bureaucrats.[37] There were two régimes in the USSR: on one side was a society arranged too hierarchically where inequalities continued to be far too noticeable, but which, under Stalin and thanks to Stalinism, had developed its own institutions, its structure, and its coherence; in spite of its internal contradictions, this society *remained upright of itself*; it evolved continuously, but its foundations were firm; it was protected against violent ruptures or dispersion by its internal agencies of liaison and mediation, the qualifications of its groups, and the importance of providing tools allowed it to *carry* the Plan, to support it instead of being pulled along by it. This society had to the fullest extent to be identical with the concrete movement of production. Over against it was a police dictatorship with no really useful purpose and an administration incapable of solving the new problems, of getting round contradictions, or of acting as arbiter in clashes of interest.

Even to the directing bureaucracy, the terror it had engendered and maintained was no longer tolerable: destruction by external forces was not more to be feared than an internal counter-revolution: no one quite believed any longer in the barbarous idol of Absolute Unity; distrust had engendered this cult, it would disappear with the disappearance of distrust. The relaxing of dictatorship would bring with it a return to corporate direction with an activating unity founded on reciprocal relationships. The new organizers, collaborators with and subordinate to Stalin, lived in contradiction: they belonged at the same time to a terrible but inefficient system which had no other reality than that of the blood it had shed, and to a society of technicians, workers whose concrete relations depended above all on the method of production and whose need was an administration of managers and arbiters.

Dangerous in external policy, all the system could do internally was to put a brake on development of production. Stalinism was a survival for whose existence it is unnecessary to look for any other reason than the very existence of Stalin. So long as he lived, above all others, as the symbol of a necessary dictatorship, the new Soviet society had no means of getting to understand itself: the policy of *blocs* kept up the cold war and, with it, the indefinite feeling that a terrible threat weighed on the USSR—the same, exactly, as had occluded the horizon since 1917; and then there was the watchword, 'The class struggle grows sharper as we get near to socialism' which justified all these calls to 'vigilance'; there was propaganda which set itself to divine everywhere the invisible presence of the enemy. The system was fed, upheld by Stalin, and Stalin, grown old, was the first victim of the system: carried to power by universal distrust, he remained the embodiment of this distrust when there was no longer any reason for its existence; to the exact extent that he felt the divergence of his own system from the society he had forged, he could no longer react except by increasing his distrust. Through having been the instigator and the agent of this 'contradiction' which had allowed the USSR to win the war, he had made himself completely incapable of directing Soviet expansion. A man is made by his *praxis*: it transforms him, uncovers through him his principles, and when it no longer bites on reality, it withdraws within him and settles in his brain, in his muscles, in the form of routine. From 1948, the new terror was a matter of routine. The 'doctors' conspiracy' had an air of familiarity, an anachronistic appearance which added to its horror; heads rolled but the real structure of society was not changed. The contrast between the old rancid pessimism of the Stalinists and the optimism of the builders increased from day to day; this young society, rightly proud of its success, was cut off from itself by a bloody and chaotic nightmare.

The principal factor in de-Stalinization was, it must be recognized, quite simply Stalin's death: a funeral veil glided to one side, uncovering Soviet society before its own eyes. An out-of-date conception of social integration disappeared at the same time as did the only man capable of imposing it. That is why the return of a dictator is impossible: the collectivity would no longer recognize itself in him; the elements of this social body welded together by multiple integrations—vertical and horizontal—brings unity into being by a complex plurality of hierarchies and of reciprocity: they have no need either of unification *from above* or through the romantic myth of incarnate unity. To have prolonged for a certain time a useless dictatorship, it would have been necessary *to be already Stalin*; but his successors, even if they had a mind to it, would have no means of imitating him: they are not sacred, they cannot become so: this positive society has liquidated idols and cults. The middle-class press has announced a hundred times that Malenkov, Khrushchev, Molotov and the rest quarrel among themselves for the succession to Stalin. That is nonsensical. After the death of an emperor, Roman generals used to quarrel among themselves for his throne: imperial power did not depend on the man who exercised it for the time being. But how could anyone canvas for the succession to Stalin *since it does not exist*? Stalin left nothing behind him unless it is a world which he made and which disowns him. De-Stalinization, to begin with, was a discovery rather than a decision: freed from the great shadow of Stalin, the leaders lost at the same time all-power and slavery; they would remain, whatever they did, immersed in the national collectivity and no one would henceforth raise himself above it. The 'retractile' policy was becoming impossible; it was necessary to perfect a policy of expansion: how give life back to the bureaucracy, the Party, those two bleeding and shrivelled agencies of Stalinist domination, without first reviving the confidence of the masses in them? But how could the masses give them its confidence if the Party did not first give them its confidence—in short, if a certain control at the base was not re-established over the apparatus? Stakhanovism was born of suspicion, of coercion, and of scarcity: it provoked hostility, passive resistance among the greater part of the workers. To increase productivity, the masses had to be made interested in it; and how interest them without first *giving* to them? A redistribution of investment could have brought the moment nearer when they realized that they were working for themselves in working for the nation. In a word, the only *possible* policy must have been completely positive, based on optimism and confidence. Stalin's USSR mistrusted others because it mistrusted itself; the new Russia was changing in policy because it was at last discovering that it could have confidence in itself; now it is strong enough, in all spheres, to open its gates proudly to the West.

For a young country sure of its strength, the worst is not always certain; it can back peace: the new policy must be developed on all planes at once; it would reach an end only in a climate of international relaxation, but it could contribute to creating that. As we know, it did not advance very far in the ways of democracy; besides democratization, as such, was the least anxiety of the leaders. Nor did it seek to get rid of the most crying inequalities, to fight wretchedness effectively: but it was, with all its deficiencies, the only true policy because it was in line with the movement which was drawing on the whole nation towards a continual rise in industrial and military potential, to hope, to the new generations' burning will to live, simple subjective expression of these extraordinary changes.

And it serves no good purpose to repeat that those who are carrying out de-Stalinization are Stalinists. What else could they be? This peculiar argument reminds me of that of the Girondins who reproached Robespierre with having, like them, been a royalist before August 10. And afterwards? It was out of Royalists that the French Revolution made the Republic and Republicans; de-Stalinization will de-Stalinize the de-Stalinators. For the alterations that have begun cannot be stopped

77

short: this society, in discovering itself, discovers also its conflicts and its defects; the working class is formed of new men who have acquired a knowledge of their powers and their rights; it is true that they have, in return, lost the traditions of the revolutionary struggle: but unless it is desired to throw everything into disorder, it is absolutely necessary to recognize that there is no question of making a revolution; inside a society founded on the socialization of the means of production, the working class can and must secure deep-rooted reforms, but the Revolution is *behind it*.[38] This class, once the terror is at an end, can no longer fail to see its contradictions: they were hidden from it in the name of Public Safety, but when the danger moves into the distance, it perceives that its practical state is opposed to its theoretical rôle as the dictatorial class; it submits to the planning which it will have to help establish. Its culture—far superior to that of no matter what proletariat—allows it to see clearly; it will formulate its problems and its demands clearly. Thus the movement building up at the heart of Soviet Society can be only a return to the sources of socialism: growth in productivity makes it essential at present that confidence be placed in the masses; and these, after having *received* culture rather than having *conquered* it, must once more discover their own activity, and themselves emancipate themselves through a struggle for reform. De-Stalinization is a policy of victory, based on the continued faith of a giant nation which, sooner or later, willy-nilly, must free all the positive forces of this society. It rejects Stalinist pessimism under its pseudo-Marxist form—it is not true that the building of socialism exacerbates the class struggle—and substitutes for it its own principles: the worst is not always certain nor man always bad; peace must be prepared for by peace. In truth, it matters little that the de-Stalinators may not be altogether liberated from Stalinism: what may be disquieting is that in the upper and medium groups a considerable number of bureaucrats remains whose interests are opposed to de-Stalinization. It is not a question, as has been alleged, of the interests of a class, not even of a circle. Stalinists are recruited everywhere, and their interests are mixed up with those of the bureaucracy considered as an agency of government: each of them is in danger of being dethroned by a specialist, in the same way that the universal machine has been dethroned by specialized machines. To the very extent that the technician represents the expression of objectivity pure and simple, he tends to bring out into relief the ineffectiveness of an authoritarian decision not based on the course of events; to the extent that tools achieve preponderance in the make-up of factory-made products, planning escapes them. The rate of growth in productivity no longer depends so much on men, and on the coercion exercised on them; from day to day, it is bound up more in the improvement of techniques and the perfecting of machines; it is the equipment itself, it might be said, which, through the mediation of engineers, defines its own possibilities and, joined to the need to interest the whole of the masses in production, determines investment policy.

In face of these new exigencies, men in position are in danger of discovering their uselessness. They defend themselves by identifying their cause with that of the Revolution. It cannot be denied that many of them are sincere; they have always conceived the revolutionary movement as a wild effort, imposed by compulsion on all and sustained by the heroism of the best: the very rough-hewn peasant who, round about 1930, rallied the industrial proletariat, had to be torn away from himself, pushed to the limit of his powers. The whole society, under the prompting of bureaucrats and Party, continued to work beyond its own possibilities; *more* was asked of it than it could give: no one is unaware that the objectives of the first five-year plans were not reached. This self-compulsion justified Stalinist pessimism and prevented it from turning into complete misanthropy: human nature was only weakness, egoism, its needs fettered planning, but the Stakhanovite was the real Stalinist hero because he rejected his own nature and represented, on the whole, the negation of a negation. In this perspective, it can well be imagined that the administration and the agencies of the State watched with some anxiety the development of a society becoming more technical from day to day: whence was the revolutionary impulse to come? If the masses absorb the heroes of labour, if technicians supervise production, won't the movement towards socialization slow down? Isn't the permanent tension of the collectivity going to slacken? Isn't there a danger of encouraging stratification into social layers? It is very significant

79

that Stalin, sortly before his death, had the chairman of the Five-Year Plan shot, accusing him of wishing to re-establish capitalism: that was the ruthless reaction of the revolutionary bureaucrat against the technician. Of course, these anxieties are vain: they simply show that the Party is necessary to the building up of socialism and that it must preserve its function as agitator and pacemaker of men *on the express condition* that the structure is to be changed. But the Stalinists of the apparatus cannot even conceive this metamorphosis; they have only one concern: to regain control of these new generations. Khrushchev is worried about the young: a week or two back, he threw out a stern warning to students, that is to say the technicians of the future. Molotov tries to intimidate artists and writers. I do not say that either of them is representative of the Stalinist bureaucrats: that is for the extra-clearsighted to decide.[39] What is certain is that they both reflect the present contradictions of Soviet society, and that they are both subject to contrary influences according to the particular moment and the actual circumstances. What is disquieting is that the existence of these Stalinist elements, still numerous and powerful, conservative and revolutionary at the same time, engenders and upholds a dangerous illusion, both externally and internally: it would seem, in fact, that Soviet bureaucracy has at its disposal a policy of change, and a spare team all ready to put it into effect. That is untrue: perhaps the team exists, but not the policy. 'Neo-Stalinism' is not viable, it was born without a head; what is called by this name is the desperate attempt of a group to defend its privileges and its prejudices. Where may that lead? To its liquidation, if we are lucky. If not, to disorderly upheavals, mistakes, crimes, war.

Unfortunately, each time the West bets on the worst, it increases the influence in the East of those who have bet on war. All farseeing men, whatever their political leanings, have said and repeated that there must be a response to the first overtures of the USSR; all have shown that great risks are involved in discouraging budding de-Stalinization. Unfortunately, the cold war has changed the structure of society among us too. Everywhere, anti-Communism has carried the conservatives to power: they are the natural allies of Stalinism. And then there are the arms manufacturers: the spectre of Peace has plunged

80

them into panic terror. Anything, but not *that*: their representatives have made haste to vote for the rearmament of Germany. Disastrous, ineffectual, this rearmament had only one advantage: it checked de-Stalinization, it reinstated the cold war. In point of fact, Khrushchev replaced Malenkov and reaffirmed the primacy of heavy industry.

But what, to begin with, weighed down the scales in favour of the Stalinists was the insurrectionary strike in Berlin. The Soviet leaders learned at one stroke two unpleasant truths: the governments of their allies had lied to them, the situation of the satellites was very different from the picture they had painted of it; de-Stalinization was not a specifically Soviet fact: it must necessarily spread to the people's democracies, and the more unbalanced their economy the graver the repercussions would be. In the USSR, victory was being de-Stalinized: the régime was stable, accepted by everyone; industry was strong, production was keeping up and was capable of increasing its rate of growth; the standard of living, still very low, was steadily rising. In the satellite countries, defeat was being de-Stalinized: if coercion were relaxed, it would mean uncovering crimes, ruinous mistakes, squandered resources, a handful of Stalinists isolated in face of hostile peoples who detested their government, the Soviets, and perhaps socialism itself. Neither Stalinism nor de-Stalinization was an article for export: in central Europe, the Soviet de-Stalinators found themselves once more jointly liable with Stalin's creatures Malenkov facilitated the return of Nagy to power, Khrushchev replaced him by Rakosi. But the new policy developed of itself, within and without the USSR: the general movement of expansion compelled the Soviets to adjust their disagreement with Tito. And how arrive at that without proclaiming that socialism can be achieved by different roads, that is to say without favouring *in all the people's democracies* those 'national Communists' whose leaders had been executed or imprisoned? At the time, the public prosecutors had sought above all to bring an action against Tito; at present Tito, victorious, demanded the quashing of all judgements. The deep contradiction in this policy leaps to the eye: the Soviet leaders upheld the Stalinists in central Europe, but, in becoming reconciled with Yugoslavia, they cast discredit on them. Khrushchev and Bulganin held a good hand in throwing back on Beria, and even on Stalin, the lies and crimes of 1950, and adding judiciously, 'We, after all, were not yet in power.' But in central Europe, those whom Stalin had compromised, those whom he had compelled to become his accomplices, were in power in 1950, and they were still there in 1955: if Rajk was innocent, a martyr, the head of the Hungarian government became an assassin. Rakosi did not seem susceptible to this pitiless logic; unfortunately for him, it compelled recognition by the whole Hungarian people. The Soviets had brought back the dictators in the waggon train of the Red Army: they had made them suspect by putting them in power, hateful by compelling them to organize a reign of terror. Now, they are disgracing them by forcing them to proclaim their crimes and to kiss the feet of Tito. None of that would have mattered very much if the criminals, immediately after confession, had been hanged. But where to find the changeover team? It existed: there were, in the prisons, men with broken teeth, nails pulled out who still retained the people's sympathy. Imprisoned by order of Stalin, they were not likely, thought the Soviet government, to become faithful allies. Without doubt, that was its greatest mistake: the old Stalinist distrust prevented it from understanding that sincere Communists would put the interests of socialism and of their country before their personal resentments, and that they would renew—on a different basis—their alliance with Russia. And whence, it will be asked, came this distrust? Were the 'Stalinists' recovering lost ground? Perhaps: Tito has not left us in ignorance that the struggle between the old bureaucracy and the representatives of the new technical administration is hot. But what counted above all was that the de-Stalinators, confronting the people's democracies, never abandoned Stalin's attitude: they did not trust them; they considered them nests of Fascists, of ignoramuses, of canting hypocrites, of camouflaged middle-class persons;[40] the workers were merely Social Democrats. The disastrous results of planning provided them with a further proof of this: it was the fault of the peoples. So that the failure of the Stalinist policy invited them to continue it.

The Twentieth Congress has a meaning which escapes us. It is enough to compare Khrushchev's official speech with his famous secret report to understand that the second had been improvised, drafted in haste; it has been compared to a kind of Shakespearean monologue, the apparent disorder of which dissimulates an order of the passions, the reading of which revealed nothing either about Stalinism or about the character of Stalin. Was it a personal effort? Did the Political Bureau entrust Khrushchev with its drafting? We do not know. Neither do we know whether it was hoped to disarm the Stalinist opposition by oversetting its idol or whether, by an unexpected higher bid, an attempt was being made to go beyond the timid efforts of the de-Stalinators in order to recover the initiative and put a brake on de-Stalinization. In any event, this ruthless manoeuvre was expressly designed for internal use: the report was read in the absence of foreign delegates; it was carefully distributed, with comments, in the factories and the *kolkhoz*es: it seems that it was communicated only to the leaders of the satellite countries. We know the result, inevitable and perhaps deliberate: it was an open secret; in the people's democracies, at the end of a week everyone knew about it. Once again the consequences of de-Stalinization in the USSR were to have their repercussions in central Europe; and that had not been the wish of either Khrushchev or the Political Bureau. The effect was terrible; it cut the Communist Parties of the people's democracies in two: the leaders and their confederates appreciated that they must disappear or compel recognition by force; but already force was deserting them: upright militants refused to support them. In Italy, Togliatti denounced the collective responsibility of the Soviet leaders: they had defended Stalin's policy or had acted as its agents. If these accusations were not carried officially by the press of the 'satellites', they had only the more force when the Poles, the Hungarians, the Rumanians took them up again on their own account in the bosom of the Party, in the factories and in the universities. By an unjust but necessary reversal, the Soviets lost their prestige through their brutal candour. They were at the same time reproached for having made the mistakes which they were denouncing, and for not having explained them. A contradictory reproach: by connecting these crimes with the very conditions of socialization in the USSR, they were made partially innocent of them. Nevertheless, it was just that which could not be forgiven them: in making a devil of Stalin, they had

83

replaced white Masses by black Masses, and had not got away from the cult of personality. The truth is that *for them and in the USSR* the operation was limited to the breaking of the idol; they had no wish whatsoever that Soviet society should appear to the Russians as the monstrous product of a deviation. But for the allied countries which had suffered so much and which had found themselves to be ruined, for the militants of central Europe who had not fabricated the cult of Stalin but had received it as a pre-fabricated product, the question of deviation cropped up first: weren't the satellites being dragged along in the orbit of a mad and eccentric planet? This time, the point of rupture had been reached: after Poznan, the Russians felt that their allies were escaping from them.

De-Stalinization marks the beginning of events in Poland, in Rumania, and in Hungary. Inversely, the USSR had to suffer the rebound of the troubles in central Europe: because it had never given up its distrust, because it had refused to envisage constructive solutions when it should have done so, the Soviet leaders had ended by taking fright, and by recourse to force. I don't know if there exists a 'Stalinist fraction' in the Political Bureau or if that whole organism swings between two extreme positions and passes from one to the other in accordance with circumstances. What is certain is that neo-Stalinism triumphed. Doubtless, the neo-Stalinists do not approve Stalin's crimes; but they resemble him in that they do the same things 'of necessity', and without noticing that they are crimes. They expect the worst and revert to the idea that a world war is probable, perhaps certain, without understanding that the balance of forces and of military potential tends towards equilibrium, that we have never been further from universal conflagration, and that it would be sufficient for them to cease to fear it for the spectre to disappear completely. But, in their formidable obstinacy, they resume verbal violence that could be tolerated when the USSR was at its weakest, without noticing that today it is absolutely intolerable. When Bulganin threatens Paris and London with atomic rockets, he does not dream of making use of these weapons; but they exist, the USSR is known to possess them. Suddenly, in his mouth, the threat takes on a reality of which, perhaps, he is not sensible. Has he even dreamed for an instant that his missiles would explode at Saint-Denis, at Saint-Ouen, at

Billancourt more often than on the roof of the Hôtel Matignon? These ill-considered utterances indirectly threatened with death the Paris proletariat, the London proletariat, at the very moment that Russian tanks were firing on the Hungarian proletariat: to be sure, they are only snarls; but they seem by their sinister thoughtlessness to augur the deliberate choice of barbarism and of absolute chaos. As we know, it has been necessary to send excuses to Nehru for these words, and for others as well.[41] There is only one way of avoiding the threatening war, and of winning it if, in spite of everything, it takes place: to be prepared for it. So that we get back to the policy of *blocs*. Is it possible that the Soviet government really believed this ineffectual Franco-British landing might be the start of a world conflict? The whole world condemned us; at the UN our representatives were put in the corner and capped with dunce's caps. It was enough for Messrs Khrushchev and Shepilov to mention their volunteers: we promised to be good. But this threat was not even necessary: a few ships sunk in the canal put us at the mercy of the USA; we would have sold our souls, and the shreds of our 'military honour' that remained, for a few drops of petroleum. Now there is no doubt that in America today the forces of war are definitely in retreat.[42] In a meeting of the Movement for Peace, a deputy put, as I have said, this significant question: 'Why do you ask our movement to get involved in Hungarian events? World peace is not threatened in Hungary—no one is ready to go to war for Budapest. It is in the Middle East that the fire may be re-lit.' Put plainly, the West washes its hands of what is happening in Hungary; but the USSR might regard the Franco-British aggression as a *casus belli*. Now, this intervention had mean but strictly limited aims: it was an attempt to *hold*, not to conquer. Eden wanted to protect the shareholders of the Suez Canal Company; Mollet, under Lacoste's influence, conceived the stupid project of crushing, at Port Said, the 'fellagahs' of Algeria. To discover in this wretched expedition, prepared without the knowledge of the USA, the proof of a hardening of the West, one must already have bet on war. What, on the contrary, it reveals are the contradictions of middle-class imperialisms and the conflicts of interest which undermine the Atlantic *bloc*. But straight away the USSR falls into a panic: rockets on Paris! volunteers in

85

Egypt! It reminds everyone that its troops can reach the Channel in forty-eight hours. What has happened to Khrushchev's paternal tone as he said to Guy Mollet, 'Set your affairs in order in Algeria. *But set them in order quickly*: no one will bother you'?

In this pessimistic perspective, the failure of the 'Plans' in central Europe worries neo-Stalinism less than does social agitation. If the Hungarian economy is limping, no matter: clamping down by authority from above will put that right. But first the rising must be crushed. Not to save socialism in Hungary, but to save it in the USSR. Not through fear of Fascist exiles or even of Social Democrats, but because of the repercussions a victory of the insurgents might have on the Rumanians, the Czechs, and above all the Germans. Success for the insurgents at Budapest, and East Germany will rise. If the Red Army intervenes, the soldiers of Bonn cross the line; it is world conflict. Neo-Stalinism fears, or pretends to fear, that this conflict will not come to birth in the Middle East; it is in Europe that it judges the situation to be explosive; for the Soviet leaders, it is in Europe that war will break out, engendered by the dislocation in their own *bloc*. Rather than face it with the satellites in revolt, they strike; they are contemptuous about destroying for fifty years the chances of socialism in Hungary so long as this bloody example paralyses the other 'satellites' with terror.

It is said that they wanted to save the world chance of socialism. I believe that. But true socialism cannot be separated from the real *praxis* of real men who struggle together against employers, 'bobbies', and sometimes the State and against soldiers. And I am still too abstract: for this is not even a movement. No: these are men on the march who form a group and carry all and sundry along with them, who organize themselves and change in so doing, who are made by history and make it. Their activity is based on their needs, and their needs are as true as they are themselves. But the socialism in whose name the Soviet soldiers fired on the masses in Hungary—I know nothing of it, I cannot even conceive it. It is not made for men or by them, it is a name given to a new form of alienation. It has been claimed that at Budapest the USSR was defending its national interests: that is both true and false. For

86

the USSR, a socialist country, national interests can never be marked off from the interests of socialism: thus the Puritan of New England never distinguished his material prosperity from the divine blessing, and took up arms to defend simultaneously God and private property. Only that does not damn *all* Soviet policy; on the contrary: in a perspective of expansion, the help supplied without *quid pro quo* to China and under-developed countries sets up socialist relations between nations while at the same time it enlarges the zone of Russian influence. But when the USSR returns to a retractile policy, socialism and nationalism, inseparably, become *State policy*. It is no longer a question of saving men, of working-class conquests, the concrete future of socialization in progress, but of preserving by force positions which, in the perspective of a world war, might be of advantage to the Soviet nation, its armies, and its armament industry. And, to be sure, the USSR must survive: that is necessary *in the cause of Communism*; all men of the Left would agree to that. But it is also necessary that it should remain socialist. In the State policy which the USSR invokes today, it is no longer possible to find anything but a vague reference to future socialism; the concrete struggle of the masses is drowned in blood in the name of a pure abstraction which is presented as essential and which throws back into insignificance and particularity all men of flesh and blood, whether or not they are workers, whether or not they are Communists. We are of those who say: the end justifies the means; adding, however, this indispensable corrective: these means define the end. The USSR is not imperialist, the USSR is peaceable, the USSR is socialist: that is correct. But when its leaders, to save socialism, throw the army of the people against an allied country; when they make those abstract beings, their soldiers, fire on workers who can no longer endure their wretchedness; when, without taking into consideration the concrete demands of the situation, they decide on their action in terms of the repercussions it might have *elsewhere*, in other countries, and, finally, in the world— they make a chimera of socialism and transform the USSR, in spite of themselves, in its own despite, into a predatory nation. The workers of all countries have too often served as a target for soldiers to agree, whatsoever reason may be advanced, that regular troops should massacre the people: at Budapest, Soviet

87

armoured cars fired in the name of socialism on all the proletariats of the world. Now, if socialism does not determine the
kind of activities which pretend to safeguard it; if it is believed
possible that it can be protected by methods related to Tsarist
repression, it becomes an indifferent and passive object, an
ideal term of reference which can be replaced, anywhere and
any time, by any other abstraction. The leaders are not unaware of this, since they lie to their people: that is a clear
recognition that they know they cannot rely on the approval of
the Soviet workers, know that they have behaved like authoritarian bureaucrats rather than like representatives of the nation:
in violating the sovereignty of Hungary, they have conjured
away that of the Soviets.

Everything is plain: in central Europe the de-Stalinators
wanted to continue Stalin's policy when, already, their attitude
in the USSR and their own declarations made this impossible.
These contradictions, their ill will, their half-concessions ended
by inducing the worst and admitting the Stalinists to be right.
These last, in temporarily taking over power again, launched
into a policy which was rash, lazy, and bloody, based on contempt for men and for human life; they artificially provoked a
return to the cold war in order to establish their power through
fear. From this point of view, the Russian intervention in
Hungary gets all its meaning: it is a localized operation within
the framework of a world war which has not yet broken out.
Now, war suspends all legality, socialist or other. Thus the sole
justification for the blow at Budapest would be evidence of
war; the blood spilled in Hungary is but a streamlet compared
with the torrents of blood that are going to flow.

Blood will not flow. Neither the Americans nor the Russians
want a hot war; the cold war has lapsed. Neo-Stalinism goes
against history. It finds its only justification—and that merely
apparent—in the people's democracies which Stalin has ruined.
Besides, everything is against it: the new Russian society, the
existence of a Communist China, even the attitude of the West.
This abstract and frantic realism is completely unreal: it has
compromised the USSR in the eyes of the world without tam-
ing Hungary. It must be condemned because facts condemn it,
and opposed by the only policy which is today adapted to
reality: that which makes man the measure of everything and

which fights against all alienations, even when they deck themselves ineptly with the name of 'socialism'; which prefers without exception negotiation to violence and reasoned solutions to massacres; which rejects the taking of an option on future war and wishes to prepare peace by acts of peace; which, finally, will dare to establish the sovereignty of the people in the Soviet Union, and national sovereignty in the 'satellite' countries. This policy of trust and expansion is exactly what was to be expected after the Twentieth Congress. Circumstances prescribe it: it is called here *democratization* and *de-Stalinization* but, whatever be its name, no other way is possible. The USSR finds itself before an alternative which it may be able to put back by a few massacres but cannot evade: either it will wind up its Stalinist bureaucracy and reconsider for itself its links with all the people's democracies, or their outbreaks will throw it into local repressions which will end preposterously in unleashing that world war which no one wants, and which everyone will have laid claim to hindering.

Merleau-Ponty wrote in *L'Express*: 'It is possible to speak fairly of the USSR, but only if it gets back into its place in history and if that *is disbelieved*, either as Good or as Evil, only if it renounces all fetishes.' That seems to be obvious. Still, we must consider where that leads us. Now, he also said, 'The only correct attitude is therefore to see Communism relatively, as a fact without privilege, as an undertaking tormented by its own contradictions, which sees only indistinctly, which has to go further.' It is on this point that we cannot agree with him. We have certainly noted, in this very article, that the building of socialism is 'tormented by its own contradictions'; if that were no longer so, history would stop. But it is also true that these contradictions are engendered from the beginning of the actual enterprise, and that, outside its objectives, this cannot be understood. Its aim is to give justice and freedom to all men; this basic intention cannot snatch it from history since, on the contrary, it is in and through history that it will come true. But nothing more is needed to differentiate it radically from all policies which aim at establishing or preserving the domination of one class over the whole of society. Each socialist nation is a peculiar undertaking which aims at constructing a world with the means available: no one can understand the people's China

89

without first seeing it and re-discovering there to the least detail the concerted effort of six hundred million men to do away with wretchedness and hunger. In what middle-class democracy is it possible to find this impulse towards the future, this conscious and sustained effort, this living unity? It is not a question of assimilating the USSR with the Good, or the proclamations of *Pravda* with absolute Truth: nothing, in the East any more than in the West, can replace these successive approximations, these discussions, these dialogues from which —slowly and by degrees—rational Truth is evolving. But, whether we like it or not, socialist building *is privileged in that*, to understand it, it is necessary to marry its movement and adopt its objectives; in short, it must be judged in accordance with what it wants and its means in accordance with its aim, while all other undertakings are estimated according to what they do not know, what they neglect or what they reject. This privilege explains another: only those who take part in it, in the East and in the West, can and should judge the socialist movement. Merleau-Ponty seems to refer by implication to some eagle's eyrie from which the evolution of people's régimes and of capitalist democracies could be jointly appraised. The answer to that is: either this transcendant point of view does not exist or else it is socialism itself, not as an absolute principle floating above the fray, but as an historical, concrete, positive, total reality. But the immense privileges of this undertaking must be paid for by the extreme severity of its judges, that is to say of its own artificers. It is loss of time to wax indignant over middle-class colonialism: we know what the system is, and we know who M. Borgeaud is: everything is so plain, and has been for so long, that anger seems to me at least optional. It is less a question of condemning it than of getting rid of it.

On the other hand, when Soviet policy puts socialism in danger, contradicts its principles and its aims, when the means it uses are in danger of destroying the ends it serves, we shall reserve all our indignation for it. It is no longer a question of fighting an enemy or getting rid of a system: a method, and the leaders who apply it, must be condemned. The greatness of their undertaking and the weight of their responsibilities deprive them all of *all mitigating circumstances*. The rascalities of colonists, capitalist exploitation have succeeded in reducing men and nations to despair; proletariats and colonized peoples have conjured up their hopes *against them*; crimes and massacres will change nothing in that. But when the Russian armour fires on blocks of flats in Budapest; when, as Césaire puts it so well, it transforms socialism into a nightmare; when the State police arrest and deport Hungarian youths and workers, it is the hope of men—their only hope—which is called into question. A young Soviet man, in a conversation reported to me by a French friend, began by accepting criticisms with a good grace and by recognizing the shortcomings of the régime. But at the end of a minute, he asked, annoyed, 'And you? What else have you to offer us?' My friend gave the answer we should all have had to make, 'Nothing. The West has nothing to offer.' But today it would be necessary to add, 'And if you Russians were to succeed in making us believe that your barbarism in Budapest is only a normal episode in the building of socialism, no one in the world would have anything to offer. To anyone.' And I quite see, in fact, that Merleau-Ponty is not very indignant about the Soviet intervention: if the USSR is worth no more and no less than capitalist Britain, then, in fact, there is hardly anything else left for us to do except cultivate our gardens. To preserve hope, it is necessary to do exactly the opposite: to recognize, in spite of the mistakes, the abominations, the crimes, the obvious privileges of the socialist camp, and to condemn with so much the more strength the policy which puts these privileges in danger.

II. 'Was this Really the Right Moment . . . '

And there is the USSR condemned! That should make you say, smiling: 'If you know how little it cares!' If I were sure of that! There are some hundreds of thousands of us in Paris who held that the attack on Suez was piracy, and who do not find the attack on Budapest very digestible. Do we count? Wouldn't half a Bulganin rocket be enough to plunge us all together into lasting silence? If that is so, how pretend that our protests are not idealistic?

Nevertheless, I am not sure that they are without effect. About the USSR, to be sure, we can do nothing: we must trust its workers, its students, those who, in the bosom of the apparatus, struggle for the elimination of Stalinism. But in France there exists a Party which will not escape, any more than we shall, from guided missiles, and whose enthusiasm would be effaced from the earth along with our protests. It is led by a political bureau which congratulated the Soviets on their happy initiative, one member of which, recently, declared himself much 'cheered up' by these exemplary massacres.

That Party is our affair, we are familiar with it, we have all, for a shorter or longer time, been its fellow-travellers: it is on this Party that we must, that we can act. And that is exactly what brings me back to my correspondents. There is one among them whom I annoy deeply. He is a progressive. It is not that he disapproves of my opinion; he even goes so far as to confide in me that he shares it: but he, at least, has the courage to be silent, and, in his judgement, it is to be regretted that I lack a similar courage. 'Is this the right moment? Anti-Communist hysteria is at its height, the crimes of our government leave us no right to condemn anyone else; we have only one task: to unite together against the war in Algeria? Sir, if this is not the moment, better say at once that the moment will never come. For, after all, suppose the Russians invade Poland tomorrow and deport Gomulka: anti-Communist hysteria would grow so violent that it would be more than ever necessary to close up round the Party. And if, the day after tomorrow, a few MIGs bombard Bucharest? That attack would provoke rage, and I think you should put down your name as ready a little later to burst with suppressed ill temper.

I understand you: these shouts, these torches, these fire-brands, these open-mouthed lynchers, all this sadism in broad daylight, the noble indignation of MM. Tixier-Vignancour and Biaggi, I agree with you that it is distasteful. And I know there are also those who would like to profit by the occasion to dissolve the CP, that this is still under consideration, and that our President of the Council, if he is one day pressed too closely by the Right-wing mob, will try to divert its frenzy by throwing it the anti-Communist bone to gnaw. Bourdet has said, and many of us have repeated, that on that day M. Mollet will find the whole Left ranged against him. That settled, I tell you quite plainly that no one is going to blackmail us any longer about Fascism. Remember: some Communist intellectuals associated themselves with a moderate protest against Soviet

92

intervention in Hungary. After the outbreak, the leaders of the CP accused them of having contributed—'in fact', it is true, and not 'intentionally'—to provoking it. Well, that too, don't you see, is repugnant. The dead and the wounded Communists have been used against their comrades. As the Party's leaders have publicly acknowledged, the USSR has been deceived a hundred times. Still, unless you accept its new mistakes with enthusiasm, objectively you are an assassin. Naturally, these are words: the petitioners have not been hanged. But the Party is not in power: remember the Slanskys, the Rajks, the Kostovs. Those occasions often began with genuine guilt; purpose came some time afterwards, then confessions, then the rope. Everyone knows, however, that M. Biaggi's troops were on duty: do you really believe that these splendid gangsters waited to begin their work for the blessing of three militants of the extreme Left, of whom they knew nothing, not even their names? Can you see them throwing themselves into the scuffle with shouts of, 'J.-F. Rolland with us'?

When we denounced the war in Indo-China, we were stabbing French soldiers in the back; when we condemn Soviet aggression, we are opening the door to Fascism and consigning the best of the militants to the butchers. The process does not vary: whatever the truth may be, it always finds something much more important that ought to be preferred to it: the morale of the troops or of the Nation, the unity of the Party, the honour of the family, in short, anything Sacred. The duty of the patriot, of the citizen, of the militant is to peddle pious lies: they are kept on the tongue like a sacramental wafer, and then they are palmed off on a neighbour, sanctimoniously. What is to be gained by that? From time to time the drain splits—for example, Khrushchev's report—and these blessed pedlars are doused with all the filth at once. Is there any point in going into more detail?

And then, believe me, these troubles will not be repeated. A Fascist demonstration might produce some dead, damage some blocks of flats; that would not shake the Party: it has seen others. On the contrary, it is well aware how to profit by it; the militants close ranks, dissensions are forgotten. The Right quickly realized that it was taking the wrong road. At first the newspapers turned benevolent smiles on these proud French youths besieging a handful of men wedged in a block of flats in the Carrefour Châteaudun; and then, on the morrow, they got the correct range: *Le Figaro* itself deplored the impetuosity, the *furia francese* of these 'students'. And the National Assembly? How promptly it took up its position against dissolution of the CP! What a majority: 453 votes to 81! It didn't embrace the CP for love, however: the deputies were saying to one another, 'Don't let's make martyrs; they will slip up of themselves.' So? Why should I keep silent?

You say the war in Algeria should be our first, our constant worry: that is true. But the Party reciprocates the politeness of the Right; the Right served the Party by its violence, the Party serves the Right by its pious lies: by what right should one who finds it natural for Russian soldiers to fire on Hungarian workers grow indignant when French soldiers fire on Arab peasants? You have foreseen the objection; you write to me, 'It is impossible to compare the two things. They are not the same.' Naturally, they are not the same: but this is no longer even a question of truth, I am speaking about the effectiveness of a campaign. As you are well aware, the Communist speaker who, before a public drawn from the people, answers his Right-wing opponents by saying, 'They cannot be compared, they are not the same thing!' has got his back to the wall and has lost the game. That is why, if there is still time, the only way of helping the Communist Party to recover its influence is to oppose its lies with the truth, as often and as long as may be necessary to convince all its militants. Several months ago, in Budapest, a Hungarian woman journalist denounced the outrageous comfort enjoyed by high officials. The article was reproduced in the English press, and Rakosi was angry: were they looking for scandal? Did they want to feed imperialist propaganda? She replied simply, 'Your luxury is the scandal, not what I said about it.' That is what I should like to reply to MM. Fajon, Stil, and Guyot: I find their lies scandalous, and I say so. But this was no revelation to anyone: anyone can buy *L'Humanité* and judge by its contents.

Now if I were to assert that, one evening in a dark alley in Montmarte, M. Stil took part in a murder, I should be putting about a gratuitous calumny which might well injure him: but everyone knows, from his own articles, that he went to Budapest, that he saw Hungarian democracy assassinated, and that he declared himself satisfied. Why therefore should I restrain myself? I can say nothing about him which would be worse than what he himself has said, do nothing more wicked than invite people to read him.

When Soviet leaders lie to their people, I cannot excuse them, but I can understand them: they are abreast of what is going on; entangled in their intestinal troubles, paralysed by their ideology, caught in the trap of a 'pacification' which calls unceasingly for new violence: even if, abruptly, the de-Stalinators carried them off, it would be necessary to imprison those responsible or to continue the lies so as to avoid dislocating the apparatus. But when André Stil calmly publishes his patter in the same columns in which others have spread patter on Rajk, on the camps, on the criminals in white shirts; when he comes out again, after so many contradictions and insults, after the rehabilitation of so many innocent people whom he used to deluge with spittle, with the same tone of serene infallibility and empty optimism, the reader is obliged to say to himself, 'This man doesn't know what is going on; the French leaders aren't abreast of what is going on.' I am acquainted with and approve the close friendship which unites them with the Russians: but, as a last resort, they are responsible only before the working-class masses of their own country. They will be found so much the more inexcusable since there is nothing to hinder them from telling the truth, and everything constrains them to do so. They are certainly not asked to condemn with violence the Soviet intervention. No, but only to enlighten their militants and their voters, to explain, to take a step backwards, not to soil their faces straight away with blood they have not even shed. What madness possesses them, then, that leads them to make themselves accomplices of this distant crime when with a word they could proclaim themselves innocent of it? Was there any need for them to drag into disrepute with them the militants who had confidence in them? Was it in truth necessary, without any real knowledge, to insult the victims? Couldn't they have avoided unveiling before all eyes the feebleness of their Marxism and the poverty of their information to the point at which they scandalized the historians of their own Party?

Well, well! For ten years they have been persuaded to accept

95

jesters' baubles as lanterns; after which, one fine day, they have brutally been made to realize that they had been made fools of. Vain lesson: they have learned nothing and forgotten nothing. Very recently, the Soviet leaders took it on themselves to put them on their guard: on the morrow of Poznan, Khrushchev spoke of Fascism and imperialism, attributed the troubles to foreign agents. Immediately the Polish government gave the lie to these assertions, and the Russian newspapers, without abandoning their thesis, lowered their tone and, in the end, dropped it. That was like a dress rehearsal of the Hungarian tragedy: the rôles and the points of view were obvious; it was easy to foresee that if Budapest rose, Khrushchev would draw attention to the presence in Hungary of Fascist commandos and the Arrow-Cross, and Nagy would make it clear to the world that the whole people supported the rising. Nothing made any difference: on the appointed day, the members of the political bureau of the French CP saw a bladder on a stick advancing towards them; they let out a unanimous shout: 'What a beautiful lantern!' and that shout reverberated in a hundred and eighty thousand throats.

That is why I say to my correspondent: yes, it is the moment, it is certainly the moment, perhaps it is even too late! That things should have come to this pass, that the same mistake, denounced a dozen times, should be reborn once again, with the same improbability, and should be proclaimed truth, the French CP must indeed be very ill; if it doesn't use the knife, gangrene will set in. How MM. Duchet, Bidault, Tixier-Vignancour will rejoice! But the men of the Left will not rejoice: the CP, from the votes it collects, remains the first party in France: putrid, it will infect the whole of the Left with pox.

What, in fact, can the non-Communist movements and groups do? To unite *without the CP* is to condemn themselves to impotence; to unite *against it* is to open the door to Fascism. One solution remains, and one only: unity of action *with it*. Now that is exactly what is made impossible by the Party's policy. For in the end, no one is deceived; the Common Front of the Left, whatever the importance of the small formations, will never come into being without a durable understanding between the two great working-class parties. For ten years, we have not stopped repeating this in these very columns, and we shall continue to repeat it. Only a *Front Populaire* can save our country: it alone can cure our colonial cankers, pull the economy out of Malthusianism, give it a new impulse, organize, under working-class control, the mass production that will raise the French standard of living; it alone can put down the foundations of a social democracy, reconquer national sovereignty, break the Atlantic *bloc*, and put French power at the service of world peace. This, the only policy that serves all French interests, the only policy that can save us from bloody risings, Fascism, and perhaps civil war, neither of the two parties is strong enough to lead it without the other. But worse than that: neither of the two parties can pull out of the crisis it is going through without the other. The SFIO has aged considerably in the last ten years: the average age of its deputies, and of its militants, continues to rise. The CP is getting older too; more slowly. It recruits less and less among the young; at the summit, the apparatus does not bring in new blood. The rivalries, the fratricidal fights, the mutual hatred of these two venerable parties: it has all ended in sclerosis. Their degeneration is such that both are criminal (M. Guy Mollet's government threw itself into a war of aggression alongside the British Conservatives; the leaders of the Communist Party give open approval to the arrest and deportation of workers); and each of them makes use of the crimes of the other to justify its own. Now, when one goes about shouting 'Suez!' and the other 'Budapest', perhaps they put their militants on the wrong scent, but by this reciprocal disqualification they throw discredit on the whole Left. We have got to recognize that our two great parties are the most despised in the world: M. Commin, representing the SFIO, left an international reunion of Social Democratic parties to the sound of boos. M. Stil made himself disliked in Poland, even more so in Budapest; at the Congress of the International CP, Duclos was coolly received. This degeneration is an expression of that of the country: in a France suffocated by a body of employers who have long been Malthusian, the social layers have become stratified; nothing changes, nothing stirs. Besides, the upheavals of industrial production drag behind them certain demographic changes, and these again lead to such changes in the working-class world that, to adapt themselves, trade-union and political organizations must also change. In France,

97

economic stagnation has produced a deep wound at the very heart of the proletariat; this wound is exploited in turn by politicians and trade-union leaders: they live by it, their partial and truncated views reflect it. It is not only a question of the mistakes of a team: the mistakes, the reciprocal hatred are a reflexion of solidified contradictions. Moreover, it is in this broken, paralysed Left, of which one half sinks into loneliness, and the other follows the policy of the Right, that we place our last hope. Let it fall a little lower still, and it means Fascism. Let it get up from its knees and unite, let it overcome internal contradictions, and France can live. Whatever happens, we must back it: the *Front Populaire* or stagnation—we must choose.

At this point my correspondent takes the floor again. 'And you really believe we shall help to stick these disjointed halves together again by throwing abuse at both at the same time?' Yes, I believe it. 'If we must hit out,' says he, 'let us hit out at the Socialist Party: as we all know very well, its leaders don't want unity. But the CP? What does it say day by day? That a united front is necessary! Just look at them: from Thorez to the least of the militants, they all hold out their hands to Guy Mollet, to Daniel Mayer, to Lacoste. Isn't that exactly what you want?' No: not altogether. I see very well that the CP clamours for unity of action, but it goes about things in such a way as to make it impossible. Let us look closely at the matter.

Since the elections, the CP has steadily followed the same policy. It was a question, in short, of achieving on the national plane the objectives followed by the USSR in the international field; the zones of Communist influence must be strengthened, expanded, extended by bringing into being a common front of the working-class parties. This policy was dictated to the USSR by the real de-Stalinization of Soviet society: it explained the 'thaw', the need for expansion of this formidable power. In France, it could have a meaning only if it was accompanied by a real de-Stalinization of the Party, that is to say by democratization and genuine expansion. What had to change, in short, was the inward structure of the CP, its relation to the masses, its links with other political and social groups. It had to give and take, to give so that it could take; it had to be sufficiently sure of itself—in the cultural domain, among others—

98

to overcome and to assimilate. Unfortunately, the Party retained
its Stalinist structure, its Stalinist leadership: the policy of expansion was at odds with its deep distrust and its retractile
attitude. The CP today is neither a party of the masses nor altogether a party of *cadres*. This formation of 180,000 militants,
rather than expand as the Italian CP has done, prefered to
contract, leaving the working class outside. Since 1948, the
Communist leaders have bet on war: the Atlantic *bloc* would
grow more aggressive from day to day; on the eve of the conflict, the French government would dissolve the Party. Their
aim has been to remain on the *qui-vive*, a fast moving, trained
group which had no wish to encumber itself with numerous
effectives, and could without difficulty pass over to clandestinity.
In France and in central Europe, Stalinization and the shrink-
age of the CPs took place between the first Marshall offer and
the second censure of Tito. In France as in central Europe, this
retraction has had the effect of cutting off the Party from the
masses: in taking away from the masses their power of holding
it in check, it lost its ability to act on them. Five million electors
voted for it every four years, but these votes cannot be considered
as exercising control: these electors give their votes 'to the
party which is furthest Left', and that does not imply that they
approve of its policy as a whole: a vote is always more or less
of a compromise. The result of this change is double: *first*, to
the extent that it made a satellite of the Party, it made it, willy
nilly, 'parliamentary'. It wins its victories, not in the factory or
in the street, but in the polling-booth, on election day. Its
strength tends to be reduced to the number of its deputies, its
activity seems to be effective only on the parliamentary plane.
But, in reality, the manoeuvres of the other parties and, in
particular, socialist treason have had as their immediate effect
the disarming of its power: whatever the majority may be to
begin with, another is very quickly formed whose only aim is
to neutralize the CP. What has it secured? Germany is being
re-armed, there is fighting in Algeria, prices rise. The members
of the Labour Party stirred up half Britain against the Franco-
British Suez expedition. And what did we do? What did the
hundred and fifty Communist deputies do? What did the Party
with five million votes do? We can say that it froze them. It
bears with enormous weight on political life, but all that means

99

to say is that those in the majority decide to vote *always taking its existence into account*. On the other hand, its evident importance and its secret isolation have the effect of keeping up and reinforcing the dictatorship of the political bureau: an abrupt invasion by the masses might distend the *cadres* or cause them to explode, but this small, petrified, ineffective system over which there is no control cannot be changed either by its own action or by the reaction of others.

This situation ought to impel it to look for a socialist alliance on the parliamentary plane because the votes of the SFIO, jointly with its own, would make it really effective without modifying its structure. Union at the base, on the contrary, would have led it to open out, to permit penetration in order the better to penetrate in its turn, to replace the precise frontiers which cut it off from the world by a sufficiently nebulous zone of transition in which Socialists and Communists would be mixed up in a rather vague way. I do not think that there would have been any occasion to speak, as Hervé did, of Right-wing opportunism and Left-wing opportunism: since Stalin's death, these ideas no longer have quite the same meaning. But I will say rather that the structure of the CP was in flagrant contradiction to its policy: as a result, it had necessarily to remain unreal and without practical effect.

The Fourteenth Congress took advantage of the Twentieth Soviet Congress to give a theoretical form to the line of conduct adopted by the political bureau. Chaper V of the resolutions insists on 'the possibilities of the peaceful transformation of a capitalist economy into a socialist economy'. But, if armed insurrection and civil war are ruled out, it is not only so that *internal* relaxation can get support from international relaxation. It is also because this theoretical change allows the substitution of unity at the top for unity at the base. In fact, the alliance of the proletariat and of the middle classes 'will transform Parliament itself from an instrument of middle-class dictatorship into an implement of the people's will'.

This resolution has been much criticized. But it would be wrong to consider it as reformist. In fact, it is not a question of securing, thanks to universal suffrage, a continuous succession of improvements which would lead imperceptibly to the disappearance of capitalism. The *Front Populaire*, carried to

100

power by the votes of peasants, workers, and intellectuals, will have to carry the radical transformation of society into effect by authority. Revolution, as an abrupt passing from a form of government that is ending to the beginning of a form of government, will be made at the seizure of power. It will, simply, have lost its character of violence. Nor do I think this revolution is inconsistent, as has been alleged, with that of the Second Congress of the Communist International. That, in fact, runs, 'Communism refuses to see one form of future society in parliamentary government. Its aim is the abolition of parliamentary government. There can be no question of making use of middle-class governmental institutions except with a view to their destruction.' The Fourteenth Congress does not dispute this: it is explicit that, in present conditions, parliamentary government can become the means of seizing power. But it takes good care not to say what the revolutionary front will do with power when it has conquered it; nothing proves that its first act will not be to suppress Parliament.

What is less theoretical and much more serious is that these new proposals confirm the disastrous practice of the CP: 'Since our parliamentary groups vote the same way in the National Assembly, why shouldn't we facilitate their task by acting in common in the countryside?'[43] In this surprising text, it is not the deep unity of interests or of conditions which tells in favour of a re-grouping of the two parties of the Left; the Socialist worker is not told that he is in the same boat as his Communist comrade and, willy nilly, engaged in the same struggle. No, but *since* the groups in Parliament vote in the same way, the workers who have elected these groups, whatever may be their divergence of views otherwise, will gain from joining forces. It is the political alliance at the top that justifies a coming together at the base. Nothing could be less Marxist. And then the argument has no effect, above all in France where, by tradition, the worker distrusts his deputy. But it is *not intended to have an effect*: it is simply a matter of favouring an electoral re-grouping that would allow a Left majority to be sent to the Assembly. The real place for establishing harmonious relations is Parliament itself. The aim of all these theoretical considerations is to persuade a Socialist government to accept Communist support officially. That explains why Thorez could allow

101

himself to speak recently of the need to 'win over the Socialist Party as a whole to unity of action'. At the base, an attempt could be made to detach the Socialist Left of the party from M. Mollet. In the Assembly, Mollet reigns: over his group and over the country. He is the 'Socialist Party as a whole'. It is with him that it is necessary to come to an understanding.

It is precisely with him that the CP will *never* come to an understanding. There is no doubt about that: the anti-Communism of the Socialists is nowhere more virulent than in the parliamentary group. In the factory, in offices, the workers are, to begin with, linked by their work and their claims; the parliamentary group, shut in on itself, is separated from the Communist group by an impassable ditch. Fear is dominant. And hatred. When a deputy of the SFIO remembers the terrible misfortunes of the Social Democratic parties in the people's democracies, he feels his hair stand on end; he goes purple with fury when he considers that his colleagues of the CP regard him quite simply as a traitor, and that their smiles, their soft glances dissemble a scorn that is never mitigated. But these major feelings could still count for nothing: there are the small ones. Electoral rivalries have considerable importance: each time the CP and the SFIO join together, it is the CP that has done a good stroke of business. The SFIO has its fiefs; it wants to hold them. The result is that the policy of the CP can be compared to a graceful but monotonous ballet: the faun runs after the nymph but never catches her. Guy Mollet is handled tactfully, and Guy Mollet remains uninterested. He rejects Communist votes or handles them with a pair of tongs. The CP voted him special powers: immediately the government turned to the Right and thanked it. Hatred and the fear of falling into the hands of the Communist deputies snatch it from the Left and draw it towards the MRP, towards the Independents. As Duverger said, it is behaving treacherously. Is the Party going to denounce this treason? Not at all: a door must be left ajar, mustn't it? *L'Humanité* makes mournful complaint: on the eve of the elections, it was hopeful of other morrows; when it is sure Mollet will have his majority, the parliamentary group abstains. Algeria is discussed, to be sure, but with moderation. So as not to lose face, the press of the Party growls a little. But it is understood that there will be no excitement. The movement for peace, very active in the time of M. Bidault and the [French] war in Vietnam, has fallen by the wayside: no national campaign, no meetings, no 'days'; its militants moan, some of them resign: no one tries to hold them back. As for the working class, the result, perhaps the aim, of this policy is that it is totally demobilized: nothing like the strikes of the Marseilles dockers, like the demonstration for the liberation of Henri Martin. The workers are sickened by the war in Algeria, but they are given no orders, no watchwords. The CP is reaping what it sowed: when it needs the masses, it will no longer find them. The failure of counter-demonstrations on November 13 does not mean only or even primarily that the workers in the CGT condemn the Soviet intervention;[44] it is first of all the mark of a kind of disorientation: the working class is abandoned to the forces of massification. Taken aback, Frenchmen of the Left do not know what to say. 'If Guy Mollet carries on this war in Algeria, and if Thorez allows it to be carried on,' think certain among them, 'perhaps after all it is right?' Some Socialists also, some moderate and fearful people in the SFIO, when they read *L'Humanité* say, 'A lot of noise about nothing.' That reassures them: a movement of the people would have encouraged them, constrained them to oppose the government; but these wordy violences, immediately eaten away by silence, give them a good conscience at very small expense. During this time, 500,000 young men are wasting their time in Algeria, when they are not wasting their health or their lives; the economy is in the doldrums; three days of out of seven, the workers are not working. Such is the result of this Ballet of the Left, in which one of the two Left-wing parties wants to embrace the other, and that other, by turning to the Right, evades the first's embrace.

And yet, two months ago, disgusted by the triflings of Guy Mollet, a few Socialist deputies themselves were led to play with the idea of a new *Front Populaire*. That was when the leaders of the CP rendered a signal service to the head of the government: they cheerfully approved of the carnage in Budapest. Indeed, M. Guy Mollet had no hope of so much; but he took full advantage of his opportunity, and not too clumsily worked up 'anti-Communist hysteria'. Those to be first attacked by it were the very men who had been thinking, only the previous day, of getting closer to the CP; these Socialists went mad: with joy because they had had a narrow escape, with fury because they had run into mortal danger. I even believe some of them, mature gentlemen as they are, were in favour of marching on the Soviet embassy. Has the political bureau even noticed that for years it has ruined the chances of a single front? Has it ever believed that these chances existed? That is not for me to decide.

You who ask me if it is the right moment to speak, consider this monstrous Party which blocks and freezes five millions of votes, demobilizes the working class, abandons mass action for parliamentary manoeuvre, denounces the war in Algeria softly in order to handle the Socialists tactfully—altogether in vain—and does not hesitate, at the same moment, to justify Socialist distrust by senseless declarations on events in Hungary: tell yourself that its attitude is no longer even that of unconditional surrender to the USSR, but that its leaders fake or mutilate Soviet texts, or defer their publication; that they hide or minimize the progress of de-Stalinization *even in the USSR*, and that they loudly extol every policy inspired by the spectre of Stalin; imagine that these same leaders no longer restrict themselves to accepting the decisions of the Soviet Union, but that they boast of influencing them; that they depend on the most Stalinist fraction of the apparatus and so contribute to reinforcing its influence and, in consequence, to the slowing down of democratization everywhere; recall, lastly, that the aim and effect of so many blunders, so many mistakes, so many acts of destruction have been to solidify, in the CP, certain anachronistic structures which were useful at the time of the cold war but today condemn it to ineffectiveness. Weigh well these blunders, which could be mortal, and tell me if it is not time, if it is not high time, that the backers of a united front denounce publicly the obstacles which prevent its being formed.

Understand me: it is necessary also to work on the Socialist Party. But the Socialist attitude is determined by the policy of the CP. The militants of the SFIO will never free themselves from the fear which gnaws at them, that the CP will continue to be this prehistoric monster, at the same time terrible and impotent. For they are very well aware that it is their treason which reduces it to impotence and, if they draw near it, it will suddenly regain its malignity. They feel themselves *relative*: their party has only three million electors; above all, events in

104

central Europe lead them to believe that they will be gobbled up. Their fears and their aversion will be dissipated only to the extent that the CP is acted on in the first place. In India, the caste system engendered insurmountable contradictions in all levels of society, but Gandhi judged it useless to take them all into consideration: it was necessary, he thought, to find the keystone of the building, and concentrate on that. As we know, he discovered it without difficulty: quite simply, it was the pariah caste. In the same way, to shatter the stratifications which threaten to transform the French Left into a caste system, it is necessary, to begin with, to act on the arrogant pariahs of our society, on the Communist untouchables. If they *first* change, everything will be saved.

(1) The CP would have done away with all pretext for the anti-Communist propaganda of M. Mollet if it had broadly and honestly provided the readers of *L'Huma* with information; if, rather than servilely copying the Soviet version, it had given its militants the means of forming an opinion; if, instead of clumsily publishing its contempt for the masses, its mouthpiece, M. Fajon, had striven to analyse *truthfully* the situation in Hungary. It will be said that I am dreaming, that that was impossible, that it would not have been tolerated by the USSR. That is true. Or rather, it is true *in France*; wasn't Togliatti saying, as lately as yesterday, 'What we would not admit is a return to the past system—intervention in internal questions of the parties ... incitement to ruptures in other parties or in the whole working-class movement—it is of little moment who suggests it ... We are against the return of all forms of centralized organization [in the international sphere]'?[45] And then what is wanted must be known: the single front or unconditional obedience to the USSR? In any event, it is impossible to try to do two things at once. It would be absurd for the Party to cut itself off from the USSR or to break with that country; it is not less preposterous that it would unreservedly submit to it. During Stalin's lifetime, the Soviet Union was *the* truth: it is so no longer. The Twentieth Congress showed under the false evidence of Stalinism a collection of lies, blunders, and mistakes; how could a brother party which refused to attribute infallibility to Stalin be required immediately to accept that of Khrushchev? Besides, the USSR is not the *blunder* either: it is

a nation which is forming itself, which is struggling in the contradictions of socialism, whose leaders sometimes see much further than we do and at other times not nearly so far. The time of revealed truths, of evangelical words has passed: in the West, a Communist Party cannot survive unless it acquires the right of free examination. Don't let us talk of Titoism: the French Party is not yet in power. It is simply a question of setting out a principle: the Communist Party is responsible only to the working class of its own country. And to adapting itself to that. From that necessarily flows the obligation of the USSR to treat Western Parties on a footing of equality. If the French leaders explain to the Soviet leaders that this is the price of the single front, wouldn't those leaders be encouraged to reconsider their links with our CP? Isn't this easing of international ties, this abandonment of 'centralism' in line with a policy of influence and expansion? True information (which is not to say 'objective'), correct and sincere appraisement, the sovereignty of the working class, equality in relations with the USSR, all that holds together. Without this first condition, the French Left is dead, the Party is mummified.

(2) The single front continues to be unattainable so long as the CP persists in seeking it at the top by an understanding between the parliamentary groups. It will be made at the base, if it is to be made one day. But, as I have shown above, so long as the Party maintains the restricted structure of a persecuted group, threatened with dissolution and preparing to take refuge in clandestinity, it is completely unfit to carry out this vast mixing which is one day to produce unity. Today its impervious partitions[46] result in the separation of the militants into incongruous groups of workers, middle-class persons, intellectuals: this diversity of formation, of interests, of surroundings calls for and justifies dictatorial authority in the apparatus; the isolation of the groups makes that easy. It is essential to break down these structures of distrust, to multiply the contacts of the militants among themselves if it is hoped one day to re-establish contact between the militants and the masses. The organization of the CP, adapted to perfection to clandestine action, is incapable, as it stands, of ensuring the broad and lively action of an officially recognized party. In so far as official tolerance may, from one day to the next, give place to persecution, this struc-

106

ture in the form of a network, must remain. But it must be counterbalanced by the multiplication of exchanges and of contacts. The dreadful charge of 'fractional activity' reinforces division into compartments; that is the cause of the reign of terror which hinders communication between men and the circulation of ideas. It is possible to condemn fractional activity, as Lenin did, on condition that 'tendencies' can come into the open within the organization of the Party. But there is no doubt that today tendencies turn into fractions because they cannot be expressed within the institutional framework of the CP. It would be possible to do away with fractions only if criticism and discussion are promoted *at all levels*. Reduced to silence in the constituent groups, condemned if he expresses himself outside them, the militant of the party of the working-class masses is in reality completely alone before the directorate, and his isolation reflects the isolation of the CP. If the Party wants to regain the support of the working-class masses, it must accept control by them. So long as the elements at the base can communicate only through the top, the CP will remain enclosed. If it wants to fuse with the masses, to give them back unity and rediscover life through them, it must go in for decompression. That is the very operation, founded on a policy of expansion, which we might call democratization. This is not the moment to consider under what form the CP can agree to the revival of tendencies: when the leaders themselves wanted to promote this, the ossification of the structure made it impossible for them to express themselves. This essential question is thus subordinate to the modifications which the Party must carry out on its own constitution if it wishes to become once more a party of the masses, and to impose through the base this single front which the SFIO persists in rejecting.

Equality in relations with the USSR, true reports, democratization, recovery of contact with the masses and their mobilization, *to begin with* against the war in Algeria: such are the necessary conditions by which the CP can restore itself to life, so that the two great working-class parties can achieve a common front. I see no difference between the one thing and the other. Each 'Left' has its problems: ours is that of working-class unification. It would be as abstract to consider the CP outside this concrete situation as to envisage it without taking into

107

account its ties with the USSR. As for ourselves, we have been debating with the Communists for a decade and more. At first with violence, later on with friendship. But our aim has always been the same: to join with our feeble strength in the realization of this union of the parties of the Left which *alone* can still save our country. Today, we turn back to the opposition: for this very simple reason that there is no other course open; the sole effect of alliance with the CP as it is, as it means to remain, would be to compromise the last chances of a single front. Our programme is clear: through a hundred contradictions, intestinal struggles, massacres, de-Stalinization is in progress; it is the only effective policy which is, at the present moment, useful to Socialism, peace, the bringing together of the working-class parties: with our resources as intellectuals, read by intellectuals, we shall try to help in the de-Stalinization of the French Party.

AUTHOR'S NOTES

¹ The French must have come up against French arms. And British. It is not so long since we were Nasser's suppliers.

² On 10 August 1792, after the rising was victorious, the crowd invaded the Tuileries; a few people tried to loot it: they were hanged. This condemnation is a political act in that it was first of all careful of the effect which these thefts would produce on the enemy, and of the advantage which counter-revolutionary propaganda would draw from them if they went unpunished. But it is part and parcel of certain values held by the people: disgust with royal luxury and consequently a refusal to profit from it, the revolutionary demand for purity, etc.

³ That he is a dictator is true. So what? An Egyptian Communist said to me, 'Nasser has put my two brothers and all my friends in jail. I need scarcely tell you that I don't exactly love him. But, in this Suez affair, he has the people behind him. And if historical circumstances had allowed a people's front to seize power, that government would have acted in the same way.'

⁴ Budapest in fact had some 1,700,000 inhabitants.

⁵ It is true that he dissolved them a fortnight later.

⁶ I must admit that I heard a fine speaker with expressionless eyes, a member of the Movement for Peace, who was scarcely affected by this first intervention. I have spoken in his presence and have dared him to prove its necessity to me. He went to the platform in an attempt to take up the challenge. 'The first intervention?' he asked with a good natured air, 'I must confess you disturb me a great deal: I have given the matter no thought. But I put it to myself, you know, that if the USSR, with all its armour, all its guns, and all its soldiers had wanted to put the lid on things at the time of the first incident, there would never have been a second.'

That is true. And I concede much more to my opponent: if the USSR had decided to try its atomic weapons on Budapest and a few working-class centres, today the Soviet leaders would not be bothered by Hungary's exasperating and tenacious resistance; the Hungarian problem would simply be one of re-populating the country. Besides, the approximate figure given by Nehru, in accordance with his ambassador's report, is known: 25,000 dead. '25,000 dead Hungarians', my *cadre* would doubtless say, 'how magnanimous! Just think: there were 9 millions available for killing, and the USSR left 8,975,000 of them alive! Of course, those who died of hunger, of cold, and those who were shot will have to be deducted from the total later. But, devil take it, that won't add up to 100,000. And you wax indignant?' This imbecile must be told that a massacre is not justified by the number of victims.

⁷ Without a doubt, that is true. But it is false since you speak of it owing to your defects of thought, your tics, your wholesale schematism. Where have you studied this new reality, the *bloc*: where have you shown what becomes of the class struggle in the perspective of this vast conglomerate undermined by its perpetual contradictions?

⁸ I appreciate that one might ask *whence* these exiles get their means of subsistence. But correctly this must be decided after, and not before, enquiry.

⁹ A Communist opponent is willing to make a concession to me: 'Rakosi, instead of hanging the innocent, would have done better to track down the counter-revolutionaries'. But that is to slander Rakosi: he found time to do both. In Hungary—even under Nagy's government—exhortations to Hungarians to be vigilant have never ceased: neither has the watch kept over the old officers of Horthy's army and the search for secret arms dumps. A quotation will be given later from a Hungarian author which shows clearly that denunciations were not rare and that the Government took them very seriously: a former officer, even if seventy-six years old, would be arrested if his neighbours accused him of possessing a gun. I do not mean to criticize these defensive measures: I say only that they render virtually impossible the secreting in dumps of arms dropped by parachute: reciprocal distrust, conflicting interests, and ancient hatreds, the encouragement given to informing—all these influences urge the peasants to keep a watch on one another. There is no doubt that they were discontented with the régime, and with collectivization: but they had their own way of fighting it: by passive resistance. They would not have tolerated the presence in their villages or their fields of armed groups the discovery of which would have led to a massacre. Nor must it be forgotten that the great plain of Hungary lends itself very little to the movements of franc-tireurs and guerrillas. Fighting today takes place in the marshes or in the narrow, mountainous region which serves the rebels as a refuge.

¹⁰ It is not altogether by chance that Rakosi suppressed the National Festival. (Imagine Maurice Thorez in power and issuing a decree that 14 July is no longer to be celebrated!) And if he demolished an old church in Budapest, the place of an annual pilgrimage, in order to erect alongside its site a monstrous statue of Stalin, that wasn't by an oversight either.

¹¹ Numerous, as I realize, even among the workers: Rakosi, in fact, had systematically 'proletarianized' them.

¹² After the trial of the Social Democrats of the Right in November 1947, and the purge of the Social Democratic Party in March 1948, Social Democracy and the CP held a congress of unification on 13 June 1948. From this resulted the 'Party of Socialist Workers' into which the *purged* Social Democratic Left had been purely and simply absorbed by the Party. For greater clarity, I shall henceforth refer to this group as the Hungarian Communist Party. The Social Democrats to whom I allude here are certain electors and certain sympathizers who maintain a Social Democratic formation without being *represented* by an autonomous group. Strangely enough, besides, after trial, purges, and fusion, the seat of the Social Democratic Party continued to exist at Budapest, a purely empty organism, without any link with these real currents. The Smallholders Party had not been dissolved either, but had

110

been absorbed into formations of the 'Single Front' type. The Hungarian Presidium (that is to say, the presidents of the Republic) is today still presided over by an old Smallholder, Dobi, whose only function is to represent, in his person, diversity of parties. But in the countryside and among the lower middle class of the towns, this Smallholder current has never diminished in strength. The *surface formations*, totally enfeoffed to the CP, and the *real political currents* no longer have anything in common. A non-Communist party may have an official *name* but it no longer exists except as a name; its reality lives on among the people because it represented certain interests, certain classes (we shall return to this), but it had lost its name and its power of expression. The enormous blunder of the CP is that it believed it was 'playing the game' by retaining some political personalities who were strangers to Communism, by giving them high office, and by presenting them, as it were in a frame, at rigged elections instead of appraising the situation and defining its own action in relation to the real circumstances: it should have realized that the depth of the non-Communist currents made it imperative that it should act *on the mass* and that meant: establish a *real* alliance with the democratic parties and fight their influence through the effects of a positive policy.

[13] In reading the Hungarian texts which *Les Temps Modernes* publishes, others will, I think, like myself, be struck by their theoretical irresolution. This Left is in a state of crisis: it has to think about itself again, to return to fundamental questions, to socialist method: but isn't that just what it is doing? Lack of resolution in thought indicates merely the impossibility of finding an alternative: it would not have taken long for these irresolute beings to get back to Marxism. Indeed, no. The Hungarian texts may be compared fruitfully with the Polish texts which we shall be publishing in our next number. Certain considerations respected even in violence by the old government of Poland, its strange wish not to go beyond limits when all limits had already been overrun, its moderation in horror, and above all a rapid but progressive evolution from the time of Poznan have allowed the new leaders to bring about reform while remaining Marxists and Communists.

[14] For Lenin, therefore, it was not a question of casting doubt on the value of this working-class spontaneity, but rather of demonstrating that spontaneity does not exist. Except, we might say, after unification, in and through the out-distancing of leaders.

[15] What one might in this connexion call 'spontaneity' would be rather the dumbness, the apparent inertia of the proletariat in Hungary about 1955: a description and an explanation of this condition will be found in the writings of Laszlo Pal, Stakhanovite driller, Bela Kiss, blacksmith, and Ervin Eisner, driller, published in *Les Temps Modernes*. This passivity—which masks profound rebellion—is the attitude adopted *provisionally* by a proletariat that has been abandoned. 'At last someone is paying attention to us', said a worker in regard to a newspaper article. Said another, 'The leaders ought to come to our homes'; a third, 'The leaders came, but invited only some fifty workers', etc. A Hungarian reporter added, 'They thirst for humanity'.

[16] Harsh raising of norms, sudden rationalization of a factory or of a whole sector of production, appearance of new machines to which the

worker has no time to adapt himself, reduced activity during the first twenty days of the month (because raw materials had not been delivered in time), followed by crushing overwork in the last ten days, etc.

[17] When I was writing these words, Kadar had not yet dared to dissolve the workers' councils. This has just been done. I amend my question, then, and I ask, 'What is this socialism which persists in destroying the instruments of control elected by the proletariat? And if it recognized them yesterday as true representatives of the people, how can it, without putting itself out of court, have their leaders arrested today? And if Zhukov congratulated the Nagy government for relying on the working class, ought he not to condemn a government which wants to gag that class? My Communist friends have sometimes shouted, 'Soviets everywhere!' That's a fine programme. Henceforth they will have to modify it a little: 'Soviets everywhere, except in Hungary!'

[18] On 24 October and the following days, he promised immunity to those insurgents who would lay down their arms.

[19] There exists in Hungary a kind of demographic equilibrium between the primary sector on the one hand and the secondary and tertiary sectors on the other. But in 1945 the Smallholders' Party received 53 per cent of the votes; it had thus gathered in a certain number of votes in urban centres. Tomorrow, it might become the party of the country people and of the lower middle class in the towns. The CP can no longer count on receiving, at the maximum, more than four or five per cent of the votes Even assuming that all other votes went to the Social Democrats, the socialist Left is in great danger of being in a minority.

[20] In Budapest, lynchings of Communists seem to have been few in number. But in the provinces there were several serious settlings of accounts. How this argument has been misused! That is because it permits recourse to the consecrated formula: 'Workers, sincere socialists, would never, never tolerate in their presence the raising of a hand against Communist comrades'. *Therefore*, the lynchers were members of the Arrow-Cross, and if you say the contrary, you are insulting the proletariat. But—is it because I have no sense of the sacred?—the validity of this reasoning escapes me. If the Communist comrade is in a position of responsibility, if his opportunism and his hardness of heart have made him an accomplice of the Rakosi terror, if he has humiliated, ill-used his subordinates, if he has made himself odious by his importance and by the privilege he has enjoyed, if he has had innocent people arrested and deported, why should workers and sincere socialists defend him? Doubtless, they would prefer him to be brought before a court of justice, but who will pass legal judgement on him in this time of violence during which authority has broken down? It would certainly be wrong to approve of these lynchings—some of which seem to have been of a sufficiently contemptible cruelty. But what is the use of censuring them? Has there ever been an innocuous revolution? A French Communist said to me, 'Put yourself in our place: our comrades are being murdered.' That is true. But Rajk and Slansky also were comrades. Did the French Communists cry out that they were being murdered? When supreme authority crushes a militant, they declare him at once to have been a traitor. When the people's vengeance is carried

112

out on one in a position of responsibility, in their eyes, it is the people who are criminal. It can be clearly seen that they have made their choice.

[21] From a source which I believe dependable, I have received this information: between 30 October and 4 November, about a hundred and forty members of the AVH were massacred in Budapest.

[22] Stefan Heym's novel, *The Eyes of Reason*, 1951, may be read with profit. This German Communist relates with a great deal of talent the story of the struggles of a great capitalist family with the Czech government and with the workers between 1945 and 1949. It will be said, 'It's only a novel'. True enough: but it makes a very sharp and very close analysis of the social struggles and of the difficulties peculiar to post-war Czechoslovakia.

[23] Integrated in the system, controlled, buying and selling at fixed prices goods supplied by the government, the small tradesman figures as the smallest unit in state controlled distribution. But so long as the number of large 'universal' chain stores cannot be increased these selling points will preserve a semblance of autonomy.

[24] It was right. The ill will and passive resistance of the collectivized peasants had had this result in Hungary, that the small property, burdened with taxes and rates, subject to the most vexatious measures, showed—all things being otherwise equal—a better return in quantity and in quality than the large collectivized undertakings. The 'flash-back' was necessary therefore, first and foremost from the simple economic point of view.

It was prudent. In the face of an all powerful adversary, the insurrection would have united the whole country. If redistribution of the land had not been ratified, the country people would have believed that the revolution was against them. In fact, thanks to the 'United Front' of all claims, the peasants helped the town insurgents. According to eye-witnesses, Budapest had never been so well supplied with fresh provisions as during the last days of October.

[25] Negotiations were still going on in Budapest between the Russian and the Hungarian military when the order to attack was given. Our own anti-Communists naturally made use of this opportunity to lay stress on Soviet perfidy. I do not believe in this perfidy: in the first place, because the strength of the means brought into play made it unnecessary. It seems rather that the different political groups in the Kremlin sought a solution of the Hungarian business at the same time and by independent routes. In the end, the advocates of repression carried the day.

[26] Those committees which Kadar wants to reconstitute today with the same elected members, and which he pretends the Gërö government thought of organizing *before 23 October*, while *Pravda* condemns their existence—in Yugoslavia.

[27] Even after the failure of planned economies in Hungary and in Poland, the proletariat deems that it has gained something which it is ready to defend in arms: in neither country has it given up socialism or allowed it to be abandoned. It is a *policy* that it has denounced (in Hungary it went so far as to condemn the Party responsible for this policy, but it remained faithful to the régime).

²⁸ To the same extent that it cuts off the leaders from the masses, it necessarily develops the only power than can ensure its realization: the police.

²⁹ Middle-class propaganda insists very cleverly on the fact that public men, amazing in their functions, have a mediocre private life just like all other lives. They are shown at home, seeing in the New Year with their wife (a very modest New Year celebration), playing with their children. Their life story is told, they are shown in youth, ambitious, champing at the bit, like all young people when, suddenly, there comes the *opportunity*...! So, in his development as in his intimate life, the leader, the great man, the star is *myself plus chance*.

³⁰ He was convinced, certain Soviet men have told me, that there would be a wave of desertions. But man does not always justify the suspicions of pessimists: no one deserted. The soldiers brought back new techniques, suggestions, criticisms, a vision of a changed world, but the idea of calling the régime in question never occurred to them.

³¹ And without a virtually inexhaustible man-power.

³² Wretchedness was such that many people did 'black' labour: that is to say, they carried on one and sometimes two supplementary jobs. As a result the real economy (based in part on clandestine labour) is, within the same structure, different from the nationalized economy. It should be added that the novelist Doudinzev describes the same situation in Moscow: workers whose pay is too low set up clandestine co-operatives.

³³ Fejtö notes very justly, 'Contrary to what usually distinguishes relations between highly industrialized powers and colonial or semi-colonial countries which serve them as sources of cheap primary commodities—here [in Hungary] a great, relatively under-developed power finds itself in a dominating position facing a country whose industrial capacity could complete its own. The weakness of the USSR compared with its economic and military needs explains why it did not hinder Hungary from developing its heavy industry which, on the contrary, it has over enlarged...' (*La Tragédie hongroise*, p. 108.)

³⁴ How many overseas Chinese rallied *through nationalism* to the people's China!

³⁵ The aggression came from North Korea, the provocation from Syngman Rhee; basic responsibility fell entirely on MacArthur. He did everything to catch China in the Korean trap. To the abstract visionaries who take the world for a chess-board and present Stalin in course of seizing the North Korean pawn to place it brutally on the square 'South Korea', I would recall that the North Koreans condemned to death and shot those of its leaders who were in power when the conflict broke out. Faced with the accomplished fact, China and the USSR could not react in the same way: the first could not compromise its young prestige by allowing an Asiatic people at its gates to be crushed, it knew only too well that Korea had been and perhaps still was the classic route of Japanese invasion; the second found itself in a jam: it had either to risk a world war or to alienate Asia by clumsy interventionism.

³⁶ We know the result (1964).

³⁷ One of the first results of 'de-Stalinization' will be the liquidation of the old myth of 'middle-class science' and 'proletarian science'. That means that

114

this society of constructors will want to withdraw its scientists from the preposterous influence of the bureaucracy. It is not a question of re-establishing science 'in its lofty dignity', as we say in France, but of putting absolutely everything at the service of technique. 'The confusing interventions of incompetent persons has made us lose too much time,' I was told by a Soviet man. The almost classic opposition between administrator and scientist or engineer is also to be noted in many of the novels published during these last years. Naturally, the administrator is a climber who does not possess the confidence of the workers and who doesn't know much outside his political catechism; the engineer, on the contrary, is a genuine and useful man because he has to do with material objects and with machines; for this reason, he is the workers' friend. This link (more or less direct) between the worker and the technician against the bureaucrat is clearly indicated in, for example, the first part of *Dégel*.

[38] This does not mean that here and there—as at Poznan or Budapest—there may not be bloody insurrections, but quite simply that the bureaucracy and the new technical administration are not classes.

[39] We know now (1964) what that decision was.

[40] Here, for instance, is a dialogue reported by Tito: it took place between him and Stalin in 1944: ' "Walter, be careful! the middle class is very strong in Serbia!" "Comrade Stalin, I do not agree with you on this point. The Serbian middle class is very weak." Stalin remained silent, knitting his brows, and the others round the table—Molotov, Zhdanov, Malenkov, and Beria—remained with their mouths agape.' Much later—convinced always, through distrust, of the power of the middle class and the weakness of his own allies—Stalin tried to persuade Tito that he ought to restore King Peter.

[41] This is one of the most ludicrous effects of the neo-Stalinist contradiction. The directing bureaucracy wants to practise the policy of retraction and of mistrust without losing the positions the policy of political expansion has conquered for it. As a result, it has become a two-faced Janus. Everything went very well when Nehru was simply an agent of the USA, simply a scoundrel: his protests could not touch Stalin, since they *proved* that Nehru was in the other camp But when, from the point of view of a positive policy, the extreme importance of India and of the Indian government was recognized, when things had gone so far that an official visit was paid to its leader, and he was invited to the USSR, when, on his side, another great Communist power, China, considered him as a possible mediator between the government in Washington and that in Peking, then it became necessary to recognize that some check on Soviet policy had to be conceded to this alien minister, to this great strange nation. Do not let us give way to any exaggeration: this check could be exercised only by talks in India, and by votes in the UN. Nevertheless, that is already formidable: Nehru's position allows him to play upon opinion. So that Stalinism *has no meaning* with reference to India: and formal condemnation of Soviet intervention has not had the effect of breaking the friendship of the Russian and Indian governments. But at the same moment the USSR turns towards the West and threatens, so that it can live down Hungary—and holds itself free to tone down its utterances in a note addressed to Nehru. As a result, these phrases have a double meaning; they

are at the same time an outburst of verbal violence and mere words, an objective reminder of Soviet power, and an uncontrolled reaction restricted to expressing the leaders' subjective mood. For it is *about subjectivity* that excuses are made: 'We are rather sharp, it is true; we sometimes say more than we need. But what do you expect? This impulse is stronger than we are: so much has been done to us!' It is one of the oddest features of the new Stalinist diplomacy: resort to the subjective as the position of withdrawal. It is necessary to the policy of expansion: it is what allows attenuation of the numerous conflicts which may be born at the time of first meetings. It is a sign of de-Stalinization: not because of the return to the subjective—which hasn't much to do with foreign policy—but *above all* because it is born of a new situation where *adaptation* is necessary. Stalin never got angry: he always maintained the same cold and incisive tone: but that was because he was cut off from the world. Certain great personages paid him visits: he never returned one of them. It is difficult to imagine him at a banquet in London provided by members of the British Labour Party!

[42] We shall try later to analyse the situation in the USA and to show its new social structures. But, for the moment, it is enough to recall that atomic missiles became, to a certain degree, a factor for peace from the moment the USSR learned how to make them. The conventional dangers of excess of armaments remain, but, at the present moment, they are less threatening. War industry has most certainly ended by becoming a key sector of the American economy (as it has also of the Soviet economy); but the danger of a crisis is provisionally diverted: inventions and technical improvements lead continually to the renovation of arms stocks, and even prevent them from being formed. The military budget remains crushing: a favourable situation, that, for disarmament negotiations. The Korean War was a test for the American as well as for the Russian government: the people made it clear they were hostile to it. Eisenhower won the election because he promised to end the struggle. In the event of an understanding, reconversion of war industries is not impossible: it can be brought about through aid of one kind and another given to the under-developed countries.

[43] Fourteenth Congress: Address to Socialist comrades.

[44] The recession of the CGT in the trade-union elections is a sharper indication of their disapproval.

[45] Speech of 9 December 1956 at the Eighth Congress of the International CP. The Italian CP is the only one that has never been cut off from the masses: its two million members give it strength and life; close to them, it finds both support and control. The French CP floats in the air.

[46] The intellectuals have no contact with the workers. Students act within student cells, teachers in school cells, the presence of a player of the tambourine or of the dining-hall boy could hardly be counted as a direct contact with the industrial proletariat. Writers, who live in general in middle-class centres, are on visiting terms with the lower middle class in their neighbourhood cell. Those who are responsible willingly reap advantage from the distrust with which the intellectuals inspire manual workers. Even in the meetings of the Movement for Peace, the man who splits hairs finds himself in opposition to the militant who canvasses from door to door.

116

TRANSLATOR'S NOTES

Arrow Cross: symbol used by the Hungarian Fascists before the Second World War.

Aurora, The: a cruiser of the Baltic fleet, 6,630 tons, 20 knots, which bombarded the Winter Palace, Petrograd (Leningrad), former residence of the tsars, during the October Revolution, 1917.

AVH: initials used in the English press to refer to the Hungarian secret state police during the rising of 1956. They stand for Állam Védelmi Hatoság (state authority of protection). According to contemporary reports in *The Times*, the force was disbanded in December 1956, and so great was its unpopularity that former members found great difficulty in getting subsequent employment.

Avon, (Robert) Anthony Eden, 1st Earl of (1897–   ): British politician, Conservative MP from 1923. Minister for Foreign Affairs 1935–1938, when he resigned through disagreement with Neville Chamberlain's policy in relation to Hitler and Mussolini; made Secretary for War by Churchill, 1940, Foreign Secretary 1940–1945, 1951–1955; Prime Minister 1955–1956, resigning after the Suez Canal Franco-British adventure (see introductory note, p. 1). Created Earl of Avon 1960.

Bardot, Brigitte (1934–   ): French film star, noted for her good looks and figure.

Beria, Lavrenti Pavlovich (1899–1953): Russian police chief, son of Georgian peasants, organizer of a Marxist study group at technical college in Baku; in the Caucasian secret police 1921–1931; secretary of the CP in Georgia, then a member of the Central Committee of the CP of the USSR. Appointed chief of state police and commissioner for internal affairs, 1938; one of a triumvirate with Malenkov and Molotov who took over supreme power in March 1953 on Stalin's death; arrested, tried secretly on a charge of treason, shot December 23, 1953.

Biaggi, Jean Baptiste (1918–   ): lawyer and politician. Born at Ponce, Puerto Rico; founder and president of the Parti Patriotique Populaire, November 1957–June 1958; co-founder of the Rassemblement pour l'Algérie Française, 1959; deputy 1958–1962. Officer of the Legion of Honour; awarded Croix de Guerre (1939–1945), Médaille de la Résistance.

Bidault, Georges (1899–   ): French politician. Captured by the Germans 1940 while serving in the army; released after eighteen months as over

117

age; organized in Paris the National Council of Resistance; foreign minister in General de Gaulle's first government, premier 1946, held various offices in subsequent governments. Opposed de Gaulle's policy in Algeria, joined the OAS (Organisation de l'Armée Secrète); went into exile 1963, returned to France 1968.

Blanqui, (Louis) Auguste (1805–1881): violent left-wing leader; opponent of both monarchical and parliamentary forms of government; spent much of his life in prison as a result of his political activities. A man of great sincerity, during his lifetime he achieved a prestige among French workers which did not survive him.

Borgeaud, Georges Henri (1887–   ): banker; born in Algiers; a counsellor for French foreign trade.

Bourdet, Clause (1909–   ): French journalist; member of the National Council of Resistance during the Second World War; arrested by the Germans and deported to Oranienburg, then Buchenwald; editor of *Combat*, 1947–1950; founder and until 1963 co-editor of *L'Observateur*.

Bulganin, Nikolai Alexandrovich (1895–   ): Russian politician. Born at Nijni Novgorod (Gorky), son of a book-keeper, he joined the CP 1917; worked with the secret police 1918–1922; director of Moscow electrical works 1927—1930; chairman of the Council of People's Commissars and head of the state bank 1938–1941; member of the military council 1941–1944; member of the Politburo 1946, Marshal of the USSR 1947; minister of defence in government set up after Stalin's death, 1953; prime minister 1955–1957; resumed Soviet relations with Tito, 1955; displaced by Khrushchev 1957.

Burnham, James (1905–   ): US writer, professor of philosophy at New York University 1929–1953; author of *The Managerial Revolution*, 1941; *The Coming Defeat of Communism*, 1950; *Containment or Liberation?* 1953; *Suicide of the West*, 1964, etc.

Césaire, Aimé Fernand (1913–   ): writer and politician; a teacher until 1945; member of the two Constituent Assemblies 1945 and 1946; elected deputy for Martinique (where he was born) 1946, 1951, 1956, 1958, 1962; a member of the Communist group in the National Assembly until 1956, then 1958–1959 of the Parti du regroupement africain et des Fédéralistes; then unattached. Published poems, *Cahier d'un retour au pays natal, Cadastra*, etc.; and a play *La Tragédie du Christophe*.

CGT = Confédération Générale du Travail (q.v.).

Commin, Pierre (1907–   ): French journalist. Joined SFIO in 1930; worked in the Resistance during the Second World War. Elected to the First Constituent Assembly 1945; in 1952 elected senator for Seine-et-Oise. He was on the committee of SFIO from 1946, and on the editorial board of *Le Populaire*.

Commune, The Paris, 1871: insurrectionary government set up in Paris March 18, 1871, following the withdrawal of the Prussians, in opposition to the government of Adolphe Thiers (q.v.) at Versailles, as a result of the rejection by the Parisians of the humiliating peace terms. The insurgents shot hostages, burned down the Tuileries and other buildings. They were defeated by troops from Versailles, and the Commune was overthrown May 27; 877 of the Versailles troops, 20,000 *fédérés* (among them women and children) were killed.

Confédération Générale du Travail: trade union organization, formed in 1895 (roughly the equivalent of the British Trades Union Congress); one of the most powerful labour bodies in the world. In the early days it was without political affiliations. Dissolved by the Germans in 1940, it was revived in 1944 and came under the domination of the CP, as a result of which a Socialist group, calling itself Confédération Générale du Travail—Force Ouvrière, and commonly referred to as Force Ouvrière or FO, broke away in 1948.

CP = Communist Party, in this work usually the Hungarian Communist Party.

Daily Worker, The: English Communist morning paper, developed in 1930 from the former *Weekly Worker*. It was banned January 1941–August 1942 on account of its anti-government policy. Its name was changed to the *Morning Star* in 1966.

'doctors' conspiracy', the, 1953: nine doctors (six said to be of Jewish origin) were alleged in January 1953 to have caused the death of two Soviet leaders, Zhdanov (q.v.) in 1948 and Shcherbakov in 1945, and to have plotted to kill others, by the deliberate use of incorrect medical treatment. Said to be paid agents of various foreign powers, they were arrested and 'confessed'. After Stalin's death on March 5, 1953, the ministry of internal security on April 3 issued a statement that, after a 'thorough investigation', the accused doctors had been completely cleared and had been released; those guilty of accusing them had been arrested.

Duchet, Roger Benoît (1904–   ): French politician and viniculturist. Senator for the Côte d'Or 1946, and subsequently re-elected a number of times; held government posts 1951–1956; political editor of *France Indépendente*.

Duclos, Jacques (1896–   ): Communist leader, member of the French CP from its foundation in 1920; helped to organize the Resistance during the Second World War; deputy 1926–1932, 1936–1940; senator 1959.

Duverger, Maurice (1917–   ): teacher of political sociology in Paris; leader writer of *Le Monde*, contributor to *L'Express*; numerous publications dealing with the French constitution, political science, etc.

Eden, Anthony: see Avon, 1st Earl of.

Express, L': weekly journal founded 1953; print 405,000 copies in 1967.

Fajon, Étienne (1906–   ): teacher, member of the Central Committee of the French CP from 1932, of its political bureau from 1945; deputy 1936–1940, 1946–1958, 1962; director of *L'Humanité* from 1958.

Figaro, Le: Paris newspaper, weekly 1854–1866, daily 1866–1942 and from 1944. Print, 1967, 485,000 copies.

Figaro Littéraire, Le: weekly literary journal, founded 1946. Print, 1967, 107,560 copies.

Five-Year Plan: form of economic planning which set a target for increase and development of production over a period of five years. The first five-year plan started in the USSR in 1927; plans continued up to and after the Second World War. The idea was subsequently adopted in developing the economies of other countries, especially those within the Soviet orbit. The targets aimed at were by no means always hit.

France Nouvelle, *La*: weekly journal of the French Communist Party, founded 1945. Print, 1967, 74,000 copies.

France-Soir: daily evening paper. It was founded in 1941 as a monthly of the Resistance (called *Défense de la France*) on the initiative of a group of students of the Sorbonne, and was financed by the industrialist Marcel Lebon. The name *France-Soir* was adopted in 1945, and it came under the control of the Hachette and Salmon-Lazareff groups. In 1953 its circulation passed the million mark. Print, 1967, 1,270,000 copies.

Front Populaire: term meaning people's front, often translated popular front which has not quite the same meaning. It was used in France to describe the alliance formed in 1934 by the Socialists, Communists, and Radicals under the leadership of Léon Blum (Socialist) and Maurice Cachin (Communist). *Front Populaire* governments (with Blum as premier 1936–1937 and again in 1938) held office 1936–1938.

Fryer, Peter James (1927–   ): British journalist and writer, correspondent of the *Daily Worker* 1949–1956; publications include *Hungarian Tragedy*; *Oldest Ally*: *A Portrait of Salazar's Portugal*.

Gandhi, Mohandas Karamchand (1869–1948): Indian leader. Born in Kathiawar, son of the prime minister of the former small state of Porbandar (absorbed in Bombay state 1948, part of Gujarat state from 1960); called to the bar by the Inner Temple, practised in the Bombay High Court, set up practice in Durban 1893; raised, and served with, an ambulance in the South African War, returned to India 1914 where he conducted a recruiting campaign for the Indian army. In 1918 began a campaign of passive resistance to British rule in India; suffered a number of terms of imprisonment and internment; attended the Round Table Conferences in 1931; helped to secure the acceptance by the Congress Party, the strongest political organization in India which he had led since 1920, of the terms for Indian independence, 1947; tried to reduce Hindu-Moslem hostility. He was shot dead by a Hindu fanatic January 30, 1948.

Garaudy, Roger (1913–   ): French politician, academic, writer. Member of the two Constituent Assemblies, 1945, 1946; deputy 1946–1951, 1956–1958; vice-president of the National Assembly 1956–1958; senator 1959—1962. Member of the political bureau of the French CP. Published *Les Sources françaises du socialisme scientifique*; *La Liberté*; *Humanisme Marxiste*, etc.

Gërö, Ernö: Deputy prime minister of Hungary, 1956, went to Russia after the suppression of the rising; believed to have returned to Hungary in 1962.

Girondins, The: political group during the French Revolution, led by Brissot, Condorcet, and others; first appeared 1791, largest group in the Assembly (180 members) 1792; attacked Robespierre, Marat, and Danton; fell from power 1793 when a number were executed and others fled the country.

Gomulka, Wladyslaw (1905–): Polish politician, imprisoned several times for revolutionary activities between the First and Second World Wars; a leading member of the United Workers Party from 1945, he was expelled for anti-Stalinist views in 1949 and imprisoned without trial 1951–1956 when he was elected first secretary of the United Workers Party.

Guesde, (Mathieu Bazile, called) Jules (1845–1922): French political leader. A Republican, he opposed the Second Empire; founded at Montpellier, 1870, a paper *Les Droits de l'Homme*, inspired by Jacobinism; was imprisoned in July, released after Sedan, defended the Paris Commune, was subsequently again convicted and fled to Switzerland where he founded a revolutionary group with tenets verging on anarchism. After spending some years in Italy, he returned to France in 1876 and became a convert to Marxism. He was a deputy 1893–1898 and 1906–1922; broke with Jaurès on the outbreak of war in 1914 and held posts in the Viviani and Briand cabinets. He remained faithful to the SFIO after the Communist group split off from it at the Congress of Tours, 1920.

Guyot, Jean Raymond (1900–): French politician. Fought in the Resistance during the Second World War, and was elected to the two Constituent Assemblies, 1945 and 1946; deputy in the first National Assembly after the war; was a member, then president of the Commission des Finances of the National Assembly; later a senator.

Hervé, Gustave (1871–1944): French journalist; had to give up a university post in 1901 following an action over his anti-militarist articles; became a lawyer 1908, and founded the Socialist paper *La Guerre Sociale*; changed from violent anti-militarism to ardent patriotism on the outbreak of war in 1914; left the Socialist party in 1916; supported Clemenceau. Inspired by Fascism, founded the National Socialist Party in 1927.

Heym, Stefan (1913–): Socialist writer. Born at Chemnitz, Germany, he went to the USA in 1933; served as an officer in the US army during the Second World War; settled in East Germany 1952 and gave up his US citizenship 1953. While in the USA, he wrote several novels (in English), among them *The Eyes of Reason*, 1951.

Hitler, Adolf (1889–1945): Austrian-born German leader. In 1921 he took over the leadership of the German Workers Party, founded by Anton Drexler; changed its name to the National Socialist German Workers' Party, and led it to the control of Germany in 1933. Proclaimed himself *Führer* and Reich chancellor in 1934. Overran in turn Austria, Czechoslovakia, western Poland; war declared on him by France and Britain 1939; invaded Russia, June 1941; declared war on USA, December 1941. Died (probably by suicide) in an underground bunker in besieged Berlin.

Horthy de Nagybanya, Nicolas Vitez (1868–1957): Regent of Hungary 1920–1944. Educated at the naval academy at Fiume, he commanded the Austrian fleet during the latter part of the First Great War, organized a White Army to fight the Hungarian soviet republic set up in 1919 under Bela Kun and defeated it, assuming power in 1920 and holding it until deposed in 1944. Captured in Bavaria by the US 7th Army, May 1, 1945, he was imprisoned until 1948 when he went to Portugal, living there until his death.

Humanité, L': French daily paper founded by Jean Jaurès in 1904 as a Socialist journal; passed under Communist control when the Communists split off from the Socialists at the Congress of Tours, 1920. Suppressed by the French government in August 1939, it was published clandestinely from the following October until August 1944 when it reappeared openly. Edited by Marcel Cachin from 1920 till his death in 1958; then by Fajon. Sometimes referred to as *L'Huma*. Print, 1967, 185,000 copies.

Jaurès, Jean Léon (1859–1914): French philosopher and politician. Elected a deputy in 1885, joined the Socialist Party 1893, becoming its parliamentary leader. Founded *L'Humanité* 1904, and was its first editor. An active Dreyfusard; apostle of international peace. Murdered July 31, 1914, by Raoul Villain (who was acquitted 1919 as irresponsible).

Kadar, Janos (1912–   ): Hungarian politician. Helped to organize resistance to the Germans during the Second World War; deputy police chief, 1945; assistant general secretary of the Hungarian CP, 1947; MP from 1945; arrested and charged with treason and Titoism, 1950; released and rehabilitated after Stalin's death, 1953; first secretary of the Socialist Workers (Hungarian Communist) Party from 1956; prime minister 1956–1958, 1961–1965.

Khrushchev, Nikita Sergeyevich (1894–   ): Russian politician. The son of a miner, he became a miner in the Donbas; joined the CP 1918, member of the Central Committee of the CP 1934, appointed to the Politburo 1938; organized guerilla activities against the Germans, 1941; made a lieutenant-general; secretary-general of the CP, 1953; denounced Stalin's policies, 1956; premier 1958–1964.

kolkoz: Russian term for a collective farm, the first of which were set up in the USSR in 1928 when peasant holdings were forcibly joined together, and mechanization was introduced, tractors and harvest machinery being supplied from a central pool. By 1936, nearly all farming in Russia was carried on on a collective basis. Farmers were allowed to keep a percentage of the produce of their land; all the rest went to the State. The system was introduced into the Soviet dominated countries of eastern Europe after the Second World War.

Korean War, 1950–1953: after the Japanese surrender in August 1945, the Japanese were expelled from Korea and the country was arbitrarily divided along the 38th parallel of North latitude, the north being held by Russian, the south by US forces. Russian troops left at the end of 1948, the last US forces in June 1949. A year later, June 1950, the North (Communist) Koreans invaded South Korea; an emergency meeting of the Security Council of the United Nations (which was being boycotted by the Russian delegation at the time) declared the invasion a breach of the peace, and UN (chiefly US) forces went to the help of South Korea.

Hostilities continued till 1953, when the North Koreans withdrew from South Korea.

Lacoste, Robert (1898–   ): French politician; active in the Resistance during the Second World War; secretary-general of industrial production under de Gaulle, 1944, and subsequently held various ministerial posts, including that of minister for economic affairs under Guy Mollet, 1956; a member of the two Constituent Assemblies, 1945 and 1946; Socialist deputy 1946–1958.

Laniel, Joseph (1889–   ): French industrialist and politician. Elected deputy 1932 and 1936; member of the two Constituent Assemblies 1945 and 1946; held various cabinet offices; awarded Croix de Guerre 1914–1918 and 1939–1945, and Rosette de la Résistance.

Lenin, Vladimir Ilyich (1870–1924): Russian revolutionary, son of a school inspector named Ulyanov and his Volga-German wife; his elder brother was hanged for taking part in a students' plot against the life of the tsar; he himself was expelled from his university (Kazan) for taking part in a students' demonstration. Practised law in Samara (Kuibishev); exiled to Siberia; escaped and went to Munich 1900; adopted name Lenin in 1901. Spent the First World War in Switzerland until the March revolution, 1917; with German help returned to Russia; overthrew the existing revolutionary government and introduced 'the dictatorship of the proletariat'. Made peace with Germany and consolidated the rule of the Soviets, remaining the autocrat of the new Russia until his death. Leninism, his interpretation of Marxism, was regarded by orthodox Communists as almost as sacred as the original master's work.

Lissagaray, Prosper Olivier (1839–1901): French journalist. After travelling in the USA, he founded in Paris the *Revue des cours littéraires*. He opposed the Second Empire, took part in the Commune, 1871, taking refuge in London after its overthrow. After the amnesty of 1880, he founded the paper *La Bataille*; he published, 1876, *Une Histoire de la Commune de Paris*.

Louis Bonaparte: see Napoleon III.

MacArthur, Douglas (1880–1964): US four-star general and administrator. Born at Little Rock, Arkansas, educated at West Point, gassed and wounded in the First World War. Commander in the Philippines 1928; US chief of staff 1930; military adviser to the Philippine government 1935. Recalled to active service 1941 and given command of US and Filipino forces in the Philippines. Forced by the Japanese to withdraw to the Bataan Peninsular, Luzon, he left Bataan March 1942, escaped to Australia and was made Allied commander-in-chief in the S.W. Pacific area, with hq in Australia. Led the Allied offensive against the Japanese in that area from September 1942 until the Japanese surrender in August 1945. Subsequently he was virtual dictator of Japan until recalled by President Truman in April 1951, having been UN commander in Korea from 1950.

McCarthyism: term for a form of political witch-hunting carried on in the USA during the 1950s by Senator Joseph Raymond McCarthy (1909–1957) who alleged that a number of persons working in the State

Department were known Communists, and so known to be by the Secretary of State (Dean Acheson). When called upon to produce names, he failed to produce one. A motion of censure was passed on him in the Senate, 1954; but his vicious campaign, based on 'guilt by association', had disastrous effects on public life, and on individuals, in the USA. One of the people he attacked was Mrs Eleanor Roosevelt.

Malenkov, Georgi Maximilianovich (1901–): Russian politician. Born in the Urals, he joined the Red Army in 1919, and after the civil war studied at the higher technical school in Moscow; secretary of Moscow CP 1930, he was appointed to the Central Committee of the CP 1939. A member of the war cabinet during the Second World War, he organized political work at Stalingrad (Volgograd) during the siege, 1942–1943. Deputy chairman of the council of ministers, 1946, he succeeded to the premiership on Stalin's death, 1953, but resigned 1955. He was expelled from the Central Committee of the CP, 1957, from the Party 1964.

Maleter, Colonel Pal: a young Hungarian Communist who commanded the Hungarian Freedom Army against the Russians in 1956. Made deputy minister of defence, he was sent as one of a delegation to negotiate with the Russians, by whom he was held.

Mao Tse-tung (1893–): Chinese leader who fought in the revolution of 1911–1912. Becoming interested in the writings of Karl Marx, he joined the Chinese CP in 1921; worked until 1927 with Chiang Kai-shek who then turned against the Communists. Mao led his followers on 'the long march' of 6,000 miles to Yenan in Shensi province where he set up a Communist government. After the defeat of the Japanese in 1945, he secured control of all the Chinese mainland, 1949, and in that year became chairman of the central government council and virtual dictator of Communist China.

maquis: the wild scrub-covered heath country of Corsica in which bandits found shelter. Young Frenchmen who took to the woods and mountains during the Second World War to avoid being conscripted for labour by the Germans when they overran formerly unoccupied France in 1942 called themselves men of the maquis; organized themselves into resistance groups, and were subsequently absorbed into the French Forces of the Interior which helped in the liberation of France, 1944.

Marat, Jean Paul (1744–1793): leader in the French Revolution. After studying medicine in Bordeaux and Paris, he practised in London for some years. He returned to Paris in 1777 as physician to the bodyguard of the Comte d'Artois (later Charles X of France). From 1786, devoted himself to politics, starting to publish in 1789 *L'Ami du Peuple*, an extremist journal. Elected to the Convention 1792, he replaced *L'Ami du Peuple* by *Le Journal de la République Françãise*, in which he attacked those not in agreement with him, including the Girondins. He was stabbed in his bath and killed by Charlotte Corday, a Girondin sympathizer: she was guillotined.

Marshall Plan: name popularly given to the proposals put forward by General George Catlett Marshall (1880–1959), US Secretary of State, in a speech at Harvard University, June 5, 1947, for economic co-operation among European countries in their own post-war recovery, with assistance from the USA. It resulted in the creation of the European Recovery Programme, 1948, which contributed much to the economic rehabilitation of post-war Europe.

Martin, Henri (1927–): sailor who in 1950 was sentenced to five years imprisonment for distributing among fellow sailors at Toulon leaflets against the (French) war in Vietnam.

Marx, (Heinrich) Karl (1818–1883): German economist, founder of international revolutionary socialism. He met, and formed a lifelong friendship with, Engels in Paris where he lived 1843–1845. In Brussels in 1847 he drew up with Engels the Communist Manifesto. He moved to London in 1849 and lived there for the rest of his life. *Das Kapital* was his chief work; vol. I appeared in 1867; vols. II and III, edited by Engels from notes left by Marx, appeared 1885–1894. His theories form the basis of Russian Communism, and so of all orthodox CPs.

massacres of 1848: a reference to the shooting down of some 1,500 workers after the insurrection in Paris in June 1848 (see *The Communists and Peace*, Jean-Paul Sartre, p. 134).

Mayer, Daniel (1909–): French journalist and politician; a member of the National Council of the Resistance during the Second World War; member of the two Constituent Assemblies, 1945 and 1946; elected deputy 1946, 1951, 1956; minister of labour 1946 and 1948 and held other ministerial posts. Chevalier of the Legion of Honour; holder of the Rosette de la Résistance and other awards.

Mendès-France, Pierre Isaac Isidore (1907–): French lawyer and politician; deputy 1932–1940, 1946–1958; held various ministerial posts under Blum and de Gaulle. Publications include *La Banque Internationale*, 1930; *Liberté, Liberté Chérie* (memoirs), 1952; *La Politique et la Vérité*, 1958; *La République Moderne*, 1962. Officer of the Legion of Honour; holder of the Rosette de la Résistance, etc.

Merleau-Ponty, Maurice (1906–1961): French philosopher, teacher, and writer whose writings were at first in sympathy with Sartre's existentialism; with Sartre he founded the review *Les Temps Modernes* in 1945; parted company with Sartre and with the review in 1953.

Mindszenty, Jossef: Hungarian name adopted in 1945 (instead of his German name) by Joseph Pehm (1892–), a Hungarian RC cleric ordained in 1915. Imprisoned in 1944 for his opposition to the Nazis, he was released when the Russians liberated Hungary in 1945 and for a time was in high favour; but his resistance to the Communist government formed in 1947 led to his re-arrest in 1948 on a number of improbable charges, of which he confessed himself guilty, and he was sentenced to imprisonment for life in 1949. Released during the 1956 rising, he took refuge in the US legation (later elevated to an embassy) when the rising was suppressed, and was still living there in 1969.

Mollet, Guy (1905–): French teacher and politician. He taught English at Arras 1936–1944; Mayor of Arras from 1945; member of the two Constituent Assemblies 1945 and 1946; elected deputy 1946,

1951, 1955, 1958, 1962; secretary-general of the Socialist Party (SFIO); minister of state under Blum and Pleven; held other government posts; delegate to the consultative assembly of the Council of Europe, 1949–1956; Officer of the Legion of Honour; Croix de Guerre, 1939–1945; Médaille de la Résistance, etc.

Molotov, Vyacheslav Mikhailovich (1890–   ): Russian politician whose original name was Scriabin. Secretary of the Central Committee of the Russian CP 1921; foreign commissar (later minister) 1939–1949; signed the Russo-German pact 1939; led the Russian delegation to the San Francisco Conference, 1945, which drew up the charter of the United Nations. Sent as ambassador to Outer Mongolia 1957–1960; expelled from the CP 1964.

MRP (Mouvement Républicain Populaire, people's republican movement): French political party formed in 1944 under the leadership of Georges Bidault (q.v.) from the Roman Catholic democratic section of the Resistance. It put up candidates for the first time at the first municipal elections held after the Liberation, April 1945, gaining control of 447 (out of 35,307) communes; secured 150 (out of 586) seats in the Constituent Assembly 1945, 167 in 1946. In the Council of the Republic, elected 1946, it had 70 (out of 315) seats; in 1948, only 18, after which it faded out.

Mussolini, Benito (1883–1945): Italian dictator. Born near Ravenna, the son of a blacksmith, he was in his early years a Socialist agitator, editor of *Avanti* 1912 till 1914, when he founded *Il Popolo d'Italia*, a patriotic journal. Following the Caporetto disaster of 1917, he set out to counter the defeatist attitude it produced in Italy by forming groups, chiefly of ex-soldiers, which adopted the Roman *fasces* as their emblem. These groups developed, in the chaotic state of post-war Italy, into the powerful Fascist Party which seized power in 1922 and established a dictatorship under Mussolini, *Il Duce* (the leader), that lasted until the Allied invasion of Italy in 1943. When the Germans surrendered in Italy, Mussolini tried to escape to Switzerland with his mistress Clara Petacci; they were captured near Dongo on Lake Como by Italian partisans, and after a ten-minutes' trial he was shot, and she with him. They were subsequently hung up by the heels in the Piazza Loreto, Milan.

Nagy, Ferenc: Prime minister of Hungary at the time of the Communist take-over in 1947. Nagy happened to be on holiday in Switzerland, and refused to return to Hungary.

Nagy, Imre (1896–1958): Hungarian Communist leader. A wounded prisoner of war in Russia at the time of the 1917 Revolution, he at once joined the CP and the Red Army, becoming a Soviet citizen. He went back to Hungary during Bela Kun's brief régime in 1919, then fled to France, returning to Hungary in 1923 to organize a clandestine CP. He was arrested in 1927, but escaped and got to Moscow where he remained until 1944 when he again returned to Hungary. He was criticized by Stalin in 1949 for holding 'incorrect views'. Deputy premier under Rakosi, he was forced to resign in 1955 and deprived of his party membership. But anti-Soviet feeling made him a national hero in October

1956 when he became premier for ten days. He was arrested by Soviet troops, tried in secret, and executed in 1958.

Napoleon III (1808–1873): Emperor of the French. A nephew of Napoleon I, he spent his youth in exile; returned to France following the February Revolution of 1848, was elected President by five to one in December that year, and ascended the throne as Emperor in December 1852. Defeated and captured by the Prussians at Sedan, 1870, he was released on the signing of peace, and spent the last two years of his life in England.

Nasser, Gamal Abdel (1918–   ): First president of Egypt. Born in Assiut province, he attended Cairo military academy and served as an infantry officer in Egypt and the Sudan, and in the fighting with newly founded Israel, 1948–1949. He led a *coup d'état* in 1952 which forced King Farouk from the throne and into exile, and in 1956 was elected president in a plebiscite. He nationalized the Suez Canal in 1956, which led to the abortive Franco-British attack in October that year on the canal zone.

Nehru, Jawaharlal (1889–1964): Indian politician and statesman. Educated at Harrow and Trinity College, Cambridge, and called to the bar by the Inner Temple in 1912, he practised in Allahabad High Court. He joined Gandhi's non-violent, non-co-operative movement in 1920, went to prison nine times between then and 1945 when he took part in the negotiations which led to the granting in 1947 of dominion status to India, the chiefly Hindu part, and Pakistan, the chiefly Moslem part, of the old British Indian empire. Nehru was prime minister of India until his death.

NEP = new economic policy (cf. Lenin's introduction of a New Economic Policy in Russia in 1921).

New Statesman, *The*: English political weekly journal founded in 1913.

October Revolution: Russian name for the Bolshevik-led rising which took place in Petrograd (Leningrad) in 1917 and was the beginning of the Union of Soviet Socialist Republics. According to the Gregorian Calendar in use in the West, it took place on November 7, but according to the Julian Calendar, still at that time in use in Russia, it occurred on October 25. It is called the October Revolution to distinguish it from the Social Democratic Revolution which had taken place in March 1917.

Pravda (Russian, truth): official daily paper of the Russian Communist Party. Started in 1912 by Lenin (then in exile), it was suppressed in 1914 by the tsarist government; it was revived after the March Revolution of 1917.

Rajk, Laszlo: Hungarian Communist, at one time foreign minister of Hungary. He was expelled from the Party as 'a spy and Trotskyite agent of foreign imperial powers' and brought to trial. He pleaded guilty to all charges and was hanged on October 15, 1949. Rehabilitated in 1956, he was given a state funeral in Budapest on October 6, 1956, and those responsible for his execution were subsequently arrested.

Rakosi, Matyas (1892–1963): Stalinist dictator of Hungary. He fled to the USSR in 1956, and was expelled from the Hungarian CP in 1962.

127

Robespierre, Maximilien Marie Isidore (1758–1794): French revolutionary. An attorney, he was a representative of the Third Estate summoned to the States General in 1789. A gifted orator and a man of extreme views, he was elected to the National Convention, 1792, in which his group overcame the Girondins. Elected in 1793 to the Committee of Public Safety, he was chiefly responsible for the Reign of Terror, becoming virtual dictator in 1794; but reaction set in. Robespierre and his associates were arrested, and on July 28 Robespierre was guillotined.

Rochet, Waldeck (1905–   ): French politician; deputy 1936–1940 and 1945–1958; re-elected 1958 and 1962. President of the Communist group in the National Assembly 1958–1959 and 1962–1964. Joint general secretary of the French CP 1961, then general secretary from 1964.

Rokossovsky, Konstantin Konstantinovich (1896–   ): Russian general. Born in Warsaw (then in Russia), he served in the tsarist army from 1914 till the Revolution, when he joined the Bolsheviks. He commanded the army defending Moscow against the Germans in 1941, played an important part in the Battle of Stalingrad (since re-named the Battle of the Volga) 1942–1943, later directed Russian operations in Poland and East Germany. Created Marshal of the Soviet Union 1944, he assumed Polish citizenship in 1949 and was minister of national defence and supreme commander of armed forces in Poland 1949–1956.

Rougemont, Denis Louis de (1906–   ): Swiss author, editor, and teacher; head of the French broadcasts of the Voice of America 1942–1943; founder and director of the European centre of culture at Geneva; teacher at the university institute of European studies at Geneva from 1963. His publications include *Politique de la Personne*, 1934; *Journal d'un Intellectuel en Chômage*, 1937; *La Part du Diable*, 1942; *Vivre en Amérique*, 1947; *Journal des Deux Mondes*, 1948; *L'Aventure Occidentale de l'Homme*, 1957.

September Massacres: Following the storming of the Tuileries Palace and the killing of the Swiss Guard by a Paris mob, the Paris Commune, dominated by Danton and Marat, seized power on August 10, 1792, and in the following month hundreds of royalist prisoners were massacred by mobs, alleged by some authorities to have been acting 'spontaneously', by others to have been incited by the Commune: these murders came to be known as the September Massacres.

SFIO = Section Française de l'International Ouvrière: name habitually given to the French Socialist Party.

Shepilov, Dmitri Trofimovich (1905–   ): Russian politician. He worked as political officer in the army under Khrushchev during the Second World War; promoted to major-general 1945; chief editor of *Pravda* 1952; official of the Central Committee of the CP; secretary of the CP 1955–1956 and May–July 1957; minister of foreign affairs June 1956–May 1957; represented the USSR at the Security Council of the United Nations, 1956; in charge of Soviet delegation to the Suez Conference, 1956; accused later in 1956 of anti-Party activities and deprived of all his offices.

Smallholders' Party: political party formed in Hungary after the abolition in 1945 of the feudal system of land tenure in that country. At the general election held that year it secured 245 seats out of 409; but in 1946 the Allies, then occupying Hungary, insisted that a coalition government should be formed, and in this the Communists (then having only 70 members in parliament) secured the ministry of the interior and other key posts, and during the winter of 1946–1947 arrested some 300 army officers and members of the Smallholders' Party whose secretary Bela Kovacs (1894–1959) was accused by the Russians of acting against the Soviet occupation forces. In 1947 the country passed under Communist domination.

Stakhanovism, Stakhanovite: Communist terms of praise for exceptional feats of industrial output, derived from the name of Alexei Grigoryevich Stakhanov (1905–   ), a miner in the Donbas who in 1935 hewed 102 tons of coal (some sixteen times the normal output) in one shift.

Stalin (from Russian *stal*, steel): name adopted by Joseph Vissarionovich Djugashvili (1877–1953), a native of (Russian) Georgia. Educated for the priesthood, he joined the Social Democratic Party in 1898 and was expelled from his seminary in 1899 for carrying on Marxist propaganda. Exiled to Siberia five times during 1903–1912, he escaped on each occasion and continued his revolutionary propaganda. Probably during the 1917 Revolution he attracted Lenin's attention; became a member of the Politburo 1917; distinguished himself during the civil war by his defence of Tsaritsyn on the Volga (renamed Stalingrad in his honour in 1928; Volgograd 1961). General secretary of the CP 1922; secured sole leadership of the Party, and of the USSR, 1927, and held it until his death.

Stalinism: the theory and practice of Communism and Communist rule as developed by Stalin. It was repudiated after Stalin's death by Khrushchev at the XX Congress of the Communist Party of the Soviet Union, 1956.

Stil, André (1921–   ): French writer and journalist, at one time a teacher. He was secretary-general of the Lille journal *Liberté* 1944–1949; editor of *Ce Soir* 1949; associated with *L'Humanité* 1950–1959. His books include *Le Premier Choc*, 1952 (awarded the Stalin prize); *Nous nous aimerons demain*, 1957; *Le Foudroyage*, 1960; *Viens danser, Violine*, 1964.

Suez Canal Company: French company founded in 1858 to construct the canal linking the Mediterranean with the Red Sea. In its later form, it was controlled by an international council of 33 (of whom 18 were French, 10 British). It continues to exist, though with the nationalization of the canal by President Nasser (q.v.) in July 1956, its function disappeared.

Thiers, (Louis) Adolphe (1797–1877): French lawyer, historian, and politician. Opposed Charles X and proposed Louis-Philippe as his successor, 1830. Minister of the interior 1832–1834; premier 1836 and 1840; leader of right-wing liberals under the Second Republic and the Second Empire; voted against declaration of war on Prussia, 1870; as head of the provisional government on Napoleon III's fall, he negotiated peace with Prussia and suppressed the Commune. Chosen first President of the Third Republic, 1871; forced to resign by a Monarchist-Radical coalition.

Thorez, Maurice (1900–1964): French coalminer who became a political leader. A member of the Socialist Party, he joined the Communist group which split off in 1920. Secretary-general of the French CP from 1930 until his death; went into hiding in 1939 to avoid military service, finding his way to Moscow; returned to France 1944; elected to the Consultative Assembly; member of successive cabinets until 1947. He suffered severe cerebral haemorrage in 1950, went to Russia to recuperate, returning 1953. Though a semi-invalid, he retained his Party post.

Tito: name adopted by the Yugoslav leader Josip Broz (1890–   ) who succeeded from 1948 in maintaining in Yugoslavia a form of Communism that deviated from the Russian form, despite Russian pressure. (Yugoslavia has no common frontier with the USSR.)

Tixier-Vignancour, Jean Louis (1907–   ): French lawyer and politician; deputy for the Basses Pyrénées 1936–1942, 1956–1958.

Togliatti, Palmiro (1893–1964): Italian journalist and politician, secretary-general of the Italian Communist Party from 1927, retaining that post while in Moscow 1929–1944. He held cabinet office after the Second World War until 1946.

Tours, Indre-et-Loire, Congress of: congress of the SFIO held in December 1920 at which there was a split between those who wished to adhere to the new Third (Communist) International and those, led by Blum and Longuet, who wanted to continue adherence to the Second International. The Communist group took with them *L'Humanité*, and a new paper, *Le Populaire*, was founded by the Socialist group.

Trotsky, Leon: name assumed by the Russian revolutionary Lev Davidovich Bronstein (1879–1940). Of Jewish parentage, he was educated at Odessa, arrested 1899 as a member of the South Russian Workmen's League and exiled to Siberia; escaped in 1902 and joined Lenin in London. President of the Saint Petersburg workers' soviet in the abortive 1905 revolution, he was arrested and exiled to Siberia for life, but escaped within six months and lived in Austria, France, and Switzerland until he joined Lenin in the Bolshevik Revolution, 1917. He organized the Red Army in the civil war of 1918–1920. After Lenin's death, he lost influence; expelled from the CP 1927; left Russia in 1929; in 1937 settled in Mexico where he was murdered.

Vietnam: country of south-east Asia, covering the former French colony of Cochin-China and the former French protectorates of Tongking and Annam. The Vietnam war referred to in this work is the French struggle 1946–1954, against the Viet-minh, the Annamese independence movement set up under the leadership of Ho Chi-minh (1892–   ) (trained in Moscow 1925–1927) during the Japanese occupation of Indo-China in the Second World War.

Waldeck-Rochet: see Rochet, Waldeck.

Yalta: seaside town in the Crimea, Ukraine, USSR, at which a conference

130

was held in 1945 attended by Winston Churchill, prime minister of the United Kingdom; Franklin D. Roosevelt, president of the USA; and Stalin, premier of the USSR. It drew up plans for the final stages of the Second World War in Europe and for the subsequent occupation of Germany; arranged for the calling of a meeting at San Francisco to prepare a charter for the United Nations; and, in a decision kept secret at the time, bound Russia to declare war on Japan two or three months after the surrender of Germany, promising the USSR, after the defeat of Japan, South (Japanese) Sakhalin, the Kurile Islands, and other benefits in the Far East.

Zhdanov, Andrei Alexandrovich (1896–1948): Russian politician, born at Mariupol, Ukraine. Joined the Bolshevik party in 1915. After holding various Party posts, he became secretary of the Central Committee of the CP in 1940, and during the Second World War was chairman of the Leningrad defence council. A close collaborator with Stalin, he was chosen to expound party policy at critical moments. He died suddenly in Moscow, and was buried at the foot of the Kremlin wall in Red Square.

Zhukov, Grigori Konstantinovich (1896–   ): Russian soldier. He served in the tsarist army during the First World War from 1915 until the Revolution in 1917, when he joined the Red Army. During the Second World War, he became chief of the general staff and vice-commissar for defence in 1941; made responsible for the defence of Moscow, planned the counter-offensive at Stalingrad (Volgograd), and co-ordinated the forces to raise the siege of Leningrad. He commissar the First White Russian Army in the advance on Berlin, 1945; made Marshal of the Soviet Union 1945; commanded the Russian occupation forces in Germany, 1945–1946. Minister of defence from 1955, he was dismissed in disgrace 1957, and expelled from the Central Committee of the CP. In 1966 he was awarded the Order of Lenin.

KING ALFRED'S COLLEGE

LIBRARY

WITHDRAWN FROM
THE LIBRARY

UNIVERSITY OF

KA 0047835 0